Everybody can play

Everybody can play

ENCOURAGING SPIRITUAL GIFTS IN CHILDREN

JOY CHALKE

Dedicated to all the children, parents and friends who have contributed to this journey of exploring the generous gifts that our Heavenly Father delights to give us. May you continue to grow and enjoy your inheritance as children of the most glorious king.

PREFACE

I have been a follower of Jesus for almost 50 years, since I was a young teenager. I've been fortunate to be part of some of the moves of God that ushered back into the body of Christ an awareness of the Holy Spirit and the gifts of the Spirit. I have been privileged to deliver teaching, training and workshops on hearing God and prophecy in many places and countries. I'm still passionate about seeing the gifts developed, so the body can function in fullness and fulfil its remit of reaching the nations with the love of Jesus.

What has thrilled my heart in recent years, is watching our church develop as a family, where all are encouraged to encounter and hear from God and where children are respected and listened to as part of the body. It is this that has now prompted me to write this book as a tool for churches and parents on how to work together to develop and use the gifts of the Spirit on a daily basis. The title is based on my belief that not only are the gifts available for children, but that we can approach their development as we would anything we want children to learn and a play based attitude is very much at the heart of children's learning. I also acknowledge the title and heart of John Wimber's teaching that 'Everybody gets to play' as something that I identify with.

My prayer is that God will show you a deeper and richer measure of his love and grace through encountering his voice as you engage with helping children on their journey with him.

CONTENTS

INTRODUCTION

In our church we talk about creating times for "encounter", what we mean by this is deliberately making space in our lives and services for individuals to engage with God's presence. In the Bible the image for God's presence is his face, and so we can consider these as times when we purposefully look at God's face, and often out of these times God speaks. But before you start imagining that it is all about sitting quietly contemplating, I should clarify that these encounters can often take place in a variety of ways when we are together and through what can sometimes seem a noisy, busy family gathering. It has happened through the creation of the expectation that God will meet with us in worship, in response, with Lego and playdough, with creative activities and through prayer. There has been

the provision of a platform for people, both children and adults, to share testimony, words, models and pictures of what they feel God has said. Alongside this we have had teaching on the gifts of the Spirit which has been followed up in small groups where activations can be practiced to develop the gifts. During lockdown these same expectations were outworked during our zoom church meetings. This book aims to encapsulate something of this journey with a clear theological background to the gifts of the Spirit; testimonies from some of those involved and practical activities or activations that can be used in families, small groups (with both children and adults) and in the larger church gathering.

I understand the gifts of the Spirit as God giving the church power to do what he has called us to do. As it says in 2 Peter 1:3, *"His divine power has given us everything we need for life and godliness through our knowledge of him who called us by his own glory and goodness."* In this context the gifts of the Holy Spirit are part of the "everything we need" to accomplish his plans for our lives. 1 Cor 12:4-11 introduces us to the fullest list of gifts given though the Holy Spirit.

> *There are different kinds of gifts. But they are all given to believers by the same Spirit. There are different ways to serve. But they all come from the same Lord. There are different ways the Spirit works. But the same God is working in all these ways and in all people. The Holy Spirit is given to each of us in a special way. That is for the good of all. To some people the Spirit gives a message of wisdom. To others the same Spirit gives a message of knowledge. To others the same Spirit gives faith. To others that one Spirit gives gifts of healing. To others he gives the power to do miracles. To others he gives the ability to prophesy. To others he gives the ability to tell the spirits apart. To others he gives the ability to speak in different kinds of languages they had not known before. And to still others he gives the ability to explain what was said in those languages. All the gifts are produced by one and the same Spirit. He gives gifts to each person, just as he decides.*

There are other passages that also mention spiritual gifts such as Romans 12:3-8 and many agree there is not really one definitive list, rather the scriptures show us the types of gifts that the Holy Spirit can bring for the good of the body.

The gifts of the Spirit are God giving the church power to do what he called us to do.

I acknowledge there is also a long theological history on whether the gifts are still for today, whether they are only given as individual gifts to one or two people and how we should use them, however, this book is not focused on this type of debate. I am of the opinion that it delights our Heavenly Father when we utilise the gifts he has prepared for us. I would encourage us all to think of what Paul says in 1 Corinthians 14:1 when he urges us to *"Follow the way of love. You should also want the gifts the Holy Spirit gives"*. The word 'want' has also been translated as 'desire' or 'earnestly desire' in other versions of the Bible suggesting a strong longing for spiritual gifts is to be encouraged. Later in 1 Cor 14:5 Paul says *"I would be delighted if you all spoke in tongues, but I desire even more that you impart prophetic revelation to others"*. In this context Paul is only talking about two gifts but it seems to suggest they are available for all who desire them. It is reasonable to think therefore that all the gifts he mentioned two chapters earlier should be available for us to pursue. We may not individually have the fullness of each gift, but we should be desiring them and looking for them to be demonstrated in our lives together as the body of Christ.

The gifts are given by the Holy Spirit, who is a person, so in essence we should start by seeking him rather than the gifts. Eph 5:18 encourages us to *"be (being) filled with the Holy Spirit speaking to one another with psalms, hymns, and songs from the Spirit"*. The use of the continuous present tense here indicates that being filled with the Spirit is not a once off event, neither does it have to be a series of big moments of encounter with deep troughs in between, but rather a lifestyle of dwelling closely with God. For this reason Jesus encouraged us to abide in him (John 15: 1-17) so that we are permanently attached to the source of life, the Holy Spirit. As Bill Johnson says "The cultivated awareness of his presence is vital... It is to be developed in the context of relationship... he is to be encountered, experienced, known, followed and affectionately embraced." Much of this happens outside of our meetings in our personal times with the Lord and we need to teach children how to talk to God and how to listen to his voice so that they are able to develop this relationship for themselves. What we want for all our children is that they develop their own experience of the reality of God's presence and love in their everyday life.

We start by seeking to know the Holy Spirit, who is a person.

The more we get to know the Holy Spirit who dwells within us, the more opportunity there is for us to experience the gifts that the Holy Spirit brings. These gifts are not just deposits that are left with us, but the outworking of his power within us, they depend upon relationship and us being able to see and hear what God is doing. Following the healing of the man at the pool of Bethesda, Jesus said in John 5:19-20;

> "Very truly I tell you, the Son can do nothing by himself; he can do only what he sees his Father doing, because whatever the Father does the Son also does. For the Father loves the Son and shows him all he does. Yes, and he will show him even greater works than these, so that you will be amazed".

If Jesus, the Son of God, only did what he saw his Father doing, how much more do we need to develop a relationship where we can see and hear the Father in order to accomplish the works he has prepared for us to do (Eph 2:10). Most of what is covered in this book is premised on the understanding that it can be actioned out of an ongoing relationship with God. It carries the expectation that God will meet us when we turn to him and is not dependent upon any feeling(s) we may think we need to have, but rather faith in what the Bible says about us as believers.

I believe the church needs to be naturally supernatural, that we need to understand that once we are born again our DNA is changed as we enter into a relationship that makes us heirs of God (John 1:12) and joint heirs with Christ (Roms 8:17). We are able then to start to live as Jesus did, day by day dependent upon guidance from his Father (by this I don't mean asking God what clothes to wear in the morning or similar tasks which we are fully able to make decisions about), but knowing the Holy Spirit's leading and prompting as we go about our daily life. Obviously we are not yet perfect, as Jesus was, and we will all make mistakes along the way, but creating an environment where we as a family learn together and learn from our mistakes will help us all grow into who God has created us to be. We need to help children develop this connected relationship with God rather than just knowledge about God, so that when they are facing sorrows, challenges and trials they can experience his loving care and presence.

There are times when a manifest anointing of the Holy Spirit comes upon someone and they do things they have not done before. An example of this is with Saul in the Old Testament in 1 Sam 10:10-11 and again in 1 Sam 19:23, where when the Spirit came upon Saul, he prophesied. These events in the life of Saul are an account of God's manifest presence, where he moves in power for his own purpose, rather than the everyday walking in relationship with God through the Holy Spirit that this book is focusing on.

God's manifest presence (Acts 4:24, 29-31) can feel like

different things to different people and seem different on different days. It can be a feeling or a simple knowing, but sometimes goes beyond that into an experience that something greater than us is making his presence known where we are. When people talk about encounters they have had with God they often list some of the following; a shared encounter of heaviness or the sense of the weight of his glory which promotes a stillness and sense of awe. Other times there is a manifestation of power with healing and signs and wonders released. The Bible is full of stories of God's presence and his encounters with his people as his deepest desire is to dwell with us and in us. While this book focuses on the abiding presence of God, I pray it also gives space for God to surprise us with his manifest presence and that he will be more and more manifest in our lives together.

As individuals and corporately as the church, we are given the privilege of being followers of God, we are called to both know him

and to seek him. I have always loved and often prayed the request that Moses prayed in Exodus 33:13 *"If you are pleased with me, teach me your ways so I may know you and continue to find favour with you"*. What I know is just a tiny fraction of the wonder of the God who created the heavens and the earth and who pours his favour and goodness upon me. The psalms also embody the heart cry of a people who long for more of this encounter with God, for example, *"As a deer longs for streams of water, so I long for you O God"* (Psalm 42:1-2). As adults we have a responsibility to introduce children to God who loves them, they need help to wonder about the mystery of God and they need to be able to reflect and talk about spiritual experiences. It is hoped that this book will provide ways of engagement with the Holy Spirit for you and your families, and provide opportunities to hear what God wants to say.

The book has been designed to give an overview of the context in which the gifts of the Spirit operate, with a biblical introduction to each one, testimonies from adults and children, as well as practical suggestions for effective and safe use of the gifts. At the end of the relevant chapters there are activities that can be used to help develop the process of hearing God for ourselves and others. These activities have been used with both adults and children in different contexts, so are well tested. I am not making any claims to originality for the activations, they have been resourced over a period of many years, what I have done here is collate how I have used them and how I think they can be introduced, often within the context of small groups in the local church. These groups have sometimes been adults only, children and parents or small groups on Sunday mornings alongside children and youth workers. If this is new to you, or you do not feel confident in hearing God take time to explore the activities yourself, allow the Holy Spirit to engage with you in new ways and be blessed as he reveals God's heart and plans for you.

Chapter 1

CREATING EFFECTIVE LEARNING OPPORTUNITIES

When I started at teacher trainer college, I was advised to keep learning new things so that I would remember what the process of learning is like. Now forty years later I have taken the opportunity to try some new things as I have just retired. I have learnt how to make friendship bracelets, tried needle felting, watercolour painting and re-learnt making bread! It brings a great sense of achievement when things go well, but equally demands a sense of resilience if you have to keep untangling threads to get the pattern correct as you weave a bracelet or the dough does not rise how you expected for that special loaf! Learning to hear God may require the same kind of determination and resilience from us all, we have to be prepared to practice, to learn from mistakes and have the courage to have another go. Creating supportive, inclusive and regular opportunities for this to happen is essential.

Having spent my working life in education I am passionate that we get things right for the children we care for, not expecting them to be perfect but giving them the time and space to try and experience new things. This is as true for spiritual experiences as it is for all other kinds of education, so understanding a little bit of how children learn can help us to create an environment that will encourage them to continue learning even if things do not go perfectly the first time round.

Obviously on a day to day basis encountering and experiencing

God happens within nuclear families, where parents and primary carers take responsibility for discipling and mentoring their children in a proactive relationship with God, helping them to bring together biblical truth and experience. But the gathered expression of church in small groups and large congregations also has a role to play. We know from the Bible that Jesus loved children; in Matt 19:14 he says *"Let the little children come to me, and do not hinder them, for the kingdom of heaven belongs to such as these"*. This verse shows me that children are included into God's plans and purposes. They are not just the future of the church, but they are part of the kingdom of God right now.

Sometimes we have to change our thinking to align it with how God's kingdom works, just as these words challenged the disciples they may now challenge us. This is partly due to our cultural norms, as much of the culture in the western world is about preparing children for the next stage of their development, rather than celebrating what they offer at their current place. In introducing children to gifts of the Spirit I am not suggesting they will operate in exactly the way we do, or think as we do. They are all at different stages of development with different characters and personalities, but the reality is they can know God and as the Bethel community say there is no junior Holy Spirit.

In Matt 18:2-6 we read;

He called a little child to him, and placed the child among them. And he said: "Truly I tell you, unless you change and become like little children, you will never enter the kingdom of heaven. Therefore, whoever takes the lowly position of this child is the greatest in the kingdom of heaven. And whoever welcomes one such child in my name welcomes me. If anyone causes one of these little ones—those who believe in me—to stumble, it would be better for them to have a large millstone hung around their neck and to be drowned in the depths of the sea."

This passage demonstrates the value Jesus puts on children being able to follow him and on his disciples making room for children in their lives. It suggests a need to be actively ensuring that children's walk with God is supported and encouraged so that they can avoid stumbling. For me this means thinking how I can effectively engage with children and help them to walk with Jesus, so they are living an abundant life. As part of this I believe it is important that they can learn to be dependent upon the guidance of the Holy Spirit for themselves. He is the one who can help them learn not to stumble or sin, so if I can help introduce him to them I will.

In taking a focus on children I am not talking about only considering their needs or even that children should be put first in our corporate gatherings. Rather, I am talking about the commitment to explore our faith together as the family of God. What I mean when we consider the value of children in our midst is that we recognise them as contributing parts of the body of Christ (1 Corinthians 12). This involves taking them seriously as those who can participate in our gatherings and as the church family we take on board our role in helping them to grow up into men and women of God. Our church has worked hard over a number of years with our morning family celebration to develop this ethos and it is hard work. However, the fruit is evident as our values and ethos were able to translate into zoom meetings during lockdown with children and families and older adults all contributing to our weekly online gatherings.

> ## We need to value children as part of the body of Christ with a contribution to make.

To include everyone in morning worship our church regularly has Lego, play-dough or paper and pens out (as well as the more traditional flags and musical instruments). Children and adults are free to engage with these activities and then there are opportunities to share and testify about what God has been saying. On one occasion over a period of several weeks some of the models the children were making were showing people in prison. The leadership of the meeting felt it important that we recognise that the Holy Spirit may be leading us and so we then had a meeting where we highlighted this aspect and included prayer for those in prison and those who were captive for their faith. On another occasion

a child had a Lego model of someone with a bad leg that led to a word of knowledge and prayer for healing. Not all models are so obviously words from God, very young children may just be building what they want to. One example was where a four year old built a picture of a swimming pool with two boys fighting. He was asked what he thought God might be saying and responded "it's not good to fight". This example was just a child playing with something that had happened in his life, as the parent confirmed the event had just taken place with his older siblings, however he had learnt the principle that God can speak to us! Creating an inclusive culture means we welcome all children to share what they make or draw, but the adults require wisdom and guidance to follow up appropriately. To begin with it was often the adults that modelled interpretations of what was made and drawn, but now many children when asked will say what God is speaking to them about through their contributions. They also may work collaboratively; with older children and younger siblings working together on the model and interpretation.

Creating a learning environment

It takes time to create a culture of contributions and engagement and it requires compromise on occasion, however I liken the process to thinking about creating a good environment for learning as that is partly what the gathered expression of church family is about. We come to learn from God and from each other and sometimes this is a messy process. Unfortunately, in my view, educational theory in the western world has been influenced by an outcomes agenda where everything is measured and tested, even for the youngest children. It is based upon children learning facts, often in a specific and discrete way and hence promotes a system of education very geared up to assessment. Many children do not thrive under this performance based process and can easily become disengaged with education and feel they have little value or worth because they are not meeting externally imposed standards from school.

These children may then be part of our church family and may be struggling to access something like reading and do not want to come somewhere on a Sunday that reminds them of what they cannot do, particularly if a learning approach to the things of God is based around listening to an adult, reading and completing an activity sheet. Yes, there are children who enjoy all these activities and we should include them, but there is also a need to be creative in increasing the range of ways children (and some adults!) can access not just biblical teaching but also the familiar activities of worship and prayer. We also need to make the church accessible for the unchurched and sometimes our rituals and routines can seem like barriers to those totally unfamiliar with traditional church culture.

We need to be creative, just as our Heavenly Father is creative.

The following are ideas of what I think makes for a good learning environment, one where children (and adults) can learn and develop their relationships with God.

1. <u>A child must feel safe and secure for learning to happen.</u> A well known psychologist Maslow, created a hierarchy of needs in which he said there are certain conditions that need to be fulfilled in order for others (such as education) to be most effective. The principles at the bottom of Maslow's Hierarchy of needs include: physiological needs - e.g. children cannot learn if they are hungry (we start we tea and toast on a Sunday!)

Safety and security are also extremely important, to establish this children do require some degree of predictability in their lives and they need to feel loved and accepted. So thinking about ways to make children feel included when they come into our corporate gatherings is important. One example of how our church did this was to establish family welcome so children were involved with their parents in saying hello and handing out news sheets. It meant that adults arriving could also greet the children and break down some of the barriers that can exist. As with most elements though the underlying principles have to come from the values and beliefs underpinning the action and a real desire for children to be included.

2. <u>Learning only happens when we are motivated.</u> Take a moment to think about your own journey with God and what motivates you to read your Bible, worship, pray, care for others, spread the love of God and share the gospel. Sometimes our motivation is intrinsic, we are totally impacted by God's love for us and pursue it because of that. Sometimes we can be extrinsically motivated by the inspiration of another person or a way of doing things that has resonance within us. Children are just the same and we want to be trying to develop those intrinsic motivations through encountering God. So while the physical environment, resources and opportunities are important and some variety and interest in ways of engagement are helpful, the real motivation is authentic relationships with God being made accessible to all.

3. <u>Mistakes are seen as learning opportunities and supported.</u> I think it is important that the environment allows people to make mistakes and does not require everything to be a polished performance. While I agree that what we offer God should reflect our best efforts, we also need to ensure that mistakes, or less than perfect contributions are acceptable as learning opportunities. Children (and adults) need to be comfortable to have a go at something knowing they will be applauded for courage rather than criticised for not getting something right. We have begun to involve children as part of the worship team, singing and playing instruments alongside adults. Some of the older children have also taken a role in hosting the meetings alongside an adult. These types of opportunities help promote a 'have a go' attitude and this is also true for gifts of the Spirit such as prophecy or words of knowledge, as it is only through practice with them that we get better. We regularly encourage encounter times following on from the word or during worship, where people are encouraged to ask God for something for someone else and go and give it to them. This does not lead to tidy meetings, but does provide opportunities for engagement and therefore growth.

4. <u>Diversity and difference are valued.</u> The environment and

the people in it recognise the individuality of those that make up the body. In other words we do not expect everybody to do things exactly the same way. This requires creating an environment that welcomes difference. One of the key things here is probably that we recognise that young children learn through play and activity rather than only direct instruction. Play may sound like a recipe for chaos, but I propose the key aspects of play that I am thinking of here are that play involves practice and experimentation and allows children time to become engaged. The environment needs to create a reason for children to want to explore and engage with the Holy Spirit and also needs to provide time and opportunity to do this at an appropriate level and with suitable support.

In later chapters we will explore some of the ways in which this can happen. It will look different in different churches and in different families, so one size does not fit all. In my experience many children love the Holy Spirit and enjoy the opportunity to be involved and contribute to the life of the church and family, it provides them with a sense of belonging and a sense of contribution and value. This can be done in many ways; encouraging children to share what they have heard from God and what God is saying and doing with them and their testimonies is only one starting point.

5. <u>Adults provide role models.</u> Authentic and genuine relationships with God are the first ingredients we need to inspire children to want to be like us. Children learn from what they see and are quick to sense what is real. Allowing space for questions and being prepared to acknowledge we may not have all the answers but can seek them together is an effective learning strategy. Cultivating a learning community which is hungry for God to move will be the best environment to see the gifts of the Spirit develop and the church to grow.

Making disciples – developing an apprenticeship model

Jesus at the end of his earthly life said to his followers :

"Go therefore and make disciples of all nations, baptising them in the name of the Father and of the Son and of the Holy Spirit, teaching them to observe all that I have commanded you. And behold, I am with you always, to the end of the age." Matthew 28:19-20 ESV.

The word disciple here means pupil or follower, if you are parents then your children are also your disciples. As members of a church family we also have a responsibility in the education and development of children, it is not just a job for the children's workers. Often at a dedication or baptism we commit ourselves to taking a role with the parents in supporting the growth and the development of the children so we have a role to play.

Jesus, in my view, employed both a traditional rabbi - disciple model and an apprenticeship model. Traditionally a disciple would follow a rabbi who would teach his students about the Hebrew Bible and the Talmud. It was about developing theoretical knowledge and wisdom in the study of the sacred writings and the way God moved, in order to guide others in how to live to please God and obey the commandments. Jesus, however, did not just teach his disciples about the kingdom of God, but also encouraged them to

engage in the same actions that he undertook. I suggest this seems to be more of an apprenticeship model (see Matt 10:8).

An example of Jesus apprenticing his disciples to do what he did is seen in Luke 10:1-23 where Jesus sends out seventy two of them, with many instructions, including in v. 8-9 the command *"When you enter a town and are welcomed, eat what is offered to you. Heal the sick who are there and tell them, 'The kingdom of God has come near to you'"*. In verse 17 the disciples were excited when they came back, having seen that they can now do what they had seen Jesus do and that even the demons were subject to his name. This is the model that we need to develop in our churches, moving from a purely intellectual way of instruction for both adults and children to one that allows for growth in practice as well.

So if we are all called to make disciples, there should be others who are learning from our experience and journey with God and our areas of expertise. The word apprenticeship comes from the French and simply means "to learn", in our everyday usage it has the more specific connotation of someone learning from a more skilled other and often relates to practical skills such as plumbers and carpenters. The clearest biblical instruction that relates to bringing up children in this way is Proverbs 22:6 *"Train up a child in the way he should go, And when he is old he will not depart from it."* The word training means to teach a person a particular skill or behaviour and would fit within the idea of an apprenticeship. Clearly there is in this model of learning the idea of acquiring hands-on experience rather than just theoretical knowledge. The study of anthropology shows that in some cultures and societies the apprenticeship model is still predominantly what children might experience, with the adults or elders in a village all sharing a responsibility to bring up children to understand the culture and norms of being an active member of their community.

Another version of this conceptualisation about apprenticeship breaks it into four progressive parts:

I do, you watch
I do, you help
You do, I help
You do, I celebrate

Clearly in this model the relationship between the one training and the one being trained is very important. It is helpful to think about how this model can work for developing the gifts of the Spirit within our churches and families. As adults we need to model what we want children to copy, but there also needs to be a consideration of how those who have specific gifts in these areas (1 Cor 12:7-11), can be utilised as part of the resource, to help everyone pursue a deeper level of engagement in the gifts of the Spirit. Everything needs to be modelled in a way that children can understand, which could mean modifying language and using less religious jargon. Obviously this four stage model also requires opportunities to be provided for helping and doing. One way we have done this is that our church runs prophetic appointments once a month, where the prophetic team offers to pray for individuals and families. Recently we have started inviting children who we see are hearing God clearly to come and be part of this team. They then get the opportunity to give words, but also to see the modelling by the adults they are with of all the other elements involved in giving prophetic words.

Creating family stories of what God has done (the power of testimony).

I believe that our individual and family stories, the testimonies of God's action in our lives, are an important part of how we learn and how we develop an atmosphere in which we expect God to move. The Bible is the story of God's involvement with his people and throughout it there is a sense of how families take part in sharing that story with the next generation. In Ex 10:2 we read; *"you may tell in the hearing of your son, and of your grandson ... how I performed My signs among them, that you may know that I am the Lord."* This is one verse of many that illustrates how the testimonies of God's actions were passed onto the next generation. As we explore God's gifts to us together we will have new stories to share and retell.

The root of the Hebrew word testimony, means 'do again', and sharing what God has done invites the atmosphere for God to move again. At our church, one member kept a record for many years of all the testimonies that were shared on a Sunday and these were placed in folders in the prayer room so they could be read and remembered and used to build faith for what God would do in the future. Understanding that *"the testimony of Jesus is the spirit of prophecy"* (Rev 19:10), helps us see how recounting the story of what God has done in our lives individually and corporately is part of creating an environment where the Holy Spirit can move in power. As we shall see in more detail later the words of God through prophecy and words of knowledge are powerful in changing what happens both immediately and/or in pointing to the future.

I suggest that we all need to recall and recount our own stories of what God has done, and perhaps make this a part of our family devotion times. Incidentally there are studies on the value of telling family stories (i.e. parents and grandparents talking about when they were young) that help to make children feel grounded and secure. So including into the family stories the testimonies of how we came to know God and how he has been with us in our lives will yield fruit in our homes. In the account of the healing of the man possessed by many demons, Jesus actually forbids him to follow him after he has been set free, but says;

> *"Go home to your people and report to them what great things the Lord has done for you, and how he had mercy on you." And he went away and began to proclaim in Decapolis what great things Jesus had done for him; and everyone was amazed. Mark 5:19-20*

This passage emphasises the importance of the individual encounters we have with God being shared in our localities, not just our churches. Family and church stories of what God has done help create a platform of faith and belief and support the moving of the Holy Spirit in our midst. This book contains a few of the stories I have experienced with the church family. I hope they encourage you to pursue your own experiences as families and communities and see how God will use the children to proclaim his word in your own lives.

Chapter 2

LISTENING TO GOD

As a child sitting in an Anglican church I remember hearing the vicar talk about the Lord God walking in the garden in the cool of the day (Gen 3:8). It captured my imagination that God would walk and talk with humans. I obviously was not listening to the sermon, but something in the picture or image stirred something within me. It was not until many years later that sitting in a prayer meeting as a teenager I discovered that not only could we talk to God in our ordinary everyday speech, but we could also hear him speaking too. Everything changed from that moment and I began my journey in understanding how God speaks to us.

Later I went to a large meeting where prophetic people were picking individuals from the audience and giving them words from God. While I took a break in the facilities, I asked God whether they could pick me out as I would love a word from him. I heard a very strong response in my spirit which was basically a question "Do you want me to speak to you directly or through someone else?" That experience brought home to me the desire of God's heart to speak to each one of us, and while I celebrate and utilise the prophetic gift I have been given, much of the emphasis in my teaching and speaking over the years has been to encourage everyone to hear God for themselves. The words of God are powerful and are spoken to accomplish his purposes not just in our lives but in the whole world (Isaiah 55:11).

"so is my word that goes out from my mouth:

It will not return to me empty,
but will accomplish what I desire
and achieve the purpose for which I sent it."

When we talk about hearing God's voice to those unfamiliar with the idea, we have to be clear that we do not usually hear God in the same way as we might hear the person next to us speaking. But understanding the reasons why he wants to speak to us and the ways he will do this is part of a growing relationship with him. Because of this I believe it is important to encourage children in their dependence on the Holy Spirit so that they are not solely reliant on others to hear for them and can grow deeper in their personal relationship with God. To help children walk a naturally supernatural life requires the adults around them to also seek to live in the Spirit. Talking and listening to God is a natural activity for anyone born again by the Spirit and not the privilege of a few people, as Paul encourages us in Galatians 5:25 *"if we live in the Spirit, let us also walk in the Spirit".*

Talking and listening to God is a natural activity for anyone born of the Spirit.

Throughout the Old Testament God spoke to and through individuals, and the scriptures demonstrate the longing of his heart for a relationship with his people. However, this was not possible for everyone in Old Testament days without an intermediary between God and the people. There were individuals who spoke to God; Abraham, Moses, and the prophets for example, who all demonstrated aspects of a relationship with God that involved listening to him. However, the prophet Jeremiah saw the picture of God's heart for more than was possible under the legal system of the old covenant. A new covenant was needed where everyone would have access to knowing God. In Jeremiah 31:33-34 God says through him;

> *"This is the covenant I will make with the people of Israel*
> *after that time," declares the Lord.*
> *"I will put my law in their minds*
> *and write it on their hearts.*
> *I will be their God,*
> *and they will be my people.*
> *No longer will they teach their neighbour,*
> *or say to one another, 'Know the Lord,'*
> *because they will all know me,*
> *from the least of them to the greatest," declares the Lord".*

In other words God's desire was to move from a position where knowledge is through an intermediary (Old Testament imagery), to a relationship where everyone can know him for themselves. Jesus is the facilitator of this relationship through his death and resurrection (John 3:16), but he is also the one who demonstrates how we can live in this relationship with the Father. In John 5:19-20 Jesus articulates the closeness of this relationship... *"for the Father loves the Son and shows him all he does."* It is the basis of this relationship that is the foundation for us hearing God speak.

On two occasions recorded in the gospels Jesus heard the audible voice of God speaking to him. Those two occasions show some commonalities about God's purposes in speaking and why he might speak to us in a similar way. The first occasion was after Jesus' baptism in Matthew 3:16-17;

> *"As soon as Jesus was baptised, he went up out of the water. At that moment heaven was opened, and he saw the Spirit of God descending like a dove and alighting on him. And a voice from heaven said, "This is my Son, whom I love; with him I am well pleased."*

The other passage is the transfiguration in Matthew 17:5;

While he was still speaking, a bright cloud covered them, and a voice from the cloud said, "This is my Son, whom I love; with him I am well pleased. Listen to him!"

The words that God speaks are virtually identical on both of these occasions although they represent very different times in Jesus' life and ministry. God speaks to Jesus about two things; his relationship with him and his feelings about him and these things are intertwined.

We know from the scriptures that straight after his baptism and this first public declaration of being God's son, Jesus went into the desert and after 40 days he was tempted. The temptation was around the identity that God had recently declared. The devil said *"If you are the son of God then..."* (Matt 27:40) For everyone, coming to an understanding of our identity as children of God is essential to being able to fulfil our role as sons and daughters of the King of Kings. Knowing who we are enables us to live out of that identity. Knowing we are deeply loved also speaks to us about the relationship that we have with God. It is important therefore that we understand that God wants to speak to us about who we are as the foundation of our relationship. He will speak about giftings and callings, but the priority must be to build those on the foundation of knowing who we are and whose we are.

I feel passionate that hearing what God feels about them is vital to help children navigate the difficult journey of growing up. Self-esteem, how we feel about ourselves, is built from a very early age and mental health charities are clear that issues such as low self-esteem are impacting the wellbeing of more and more children and young people. Children are bombarded through social media about expectations of what they should look like and what they should be doing. Peer pressure and bullying is rampant in both the virtual and real worlds of children and powerful in damaging self-esteem. This can lead to conflict and struggle over who they are and what they feel about themselves. It is important they have help to develop tools that enable them to disarm the power of the lies of the enemy that would seek to undermine their value and worth. The truth that comes from hearing what God thinks about them is one of these tools. Helping children to hear what God thinks of them and then teaching them how to use those words to fight the negative experiences and feelings that occur in their day to day lives is crucial.

How to Listen to God

The Bible is very clear that if we are following Jesus we can learn what his voice sounds like and we can all hear God for ourselves. In John 10:27 Jesus says *"My sheep listen to my voice; I know them, they follow me."* He is the Good Shepherd (John 10:11) who is looking after his flock, so he wants us to know him. Imagine two flocks of sheep coming together at a watering hole, they all mill around having a drink and generally getting muddled up. How are the shepherds going to sort them out? Well, if the sheep know the voice of their own shepherd, they will separate themselves out and follow after him as he calls to them. This illustration is a picture of how Jesus wants to direct us in our daily walk with him through hearing his voice.

We are learning all the time how to listen more closely, but it is good to make sure we have a clear foundation to build on so we can help others to listen and hear God as well, whatever age they are. Bill Johnson in his book *Experience the impossible* illustrates this, "All of us hear God's voice. We could not be saved otherwise. He called us to himself, and we responded...it is a divinely given grace to hear God's voice." He goes on to say we should not compare ourselves with others who may appear to hear better, as it is about our heart attitude. We need to desire to hear him and make space and time in his presence to do so. Engaging with the scriptures that indicate we are the children of God will help us build receptive and expectant hearts. (e.g. *"Beloved, now we are children of God..."* 1 John 3:2).

Sometimes we can see how spiritual principles work by looking at the natural world - it is after all his creation. It may help to think about how young children learn to talk. Imagine a young child with a parent. Much of the communication they have with each other is non-verbal through shared gaze and physical contact. The first messages they receive from their parents they do not understand as words and sentences, but they do understand the love and affection of the tone that makes them feel safe and secure, particularly as they will often be spoken to while they are being held securely and safely. Similarly, when our Heavenly Father begins to speak to us he will be telling us of his love and affection for us. We then gradually learn to distinguish words and meanings. We grow in our understanding and the accuracy with which we hear. It is not instant but develops. The Holy Spirit is the one who makes language acquisition possible as he gives us a direct internal link with the language of heaven. Part of his role is to lead us into truth (John 14:7) and we have to learn how to discern and hear that voice.

When we become Christians the Holy Spirit comes to live within us, it is the Holy Spirit that reveals the voice of God to us. It is God in us speaking to us. Children are born with the capacity to learn any language, but the brain tunes in to what is heard most often, therefore it is important to think about what we are listening to and what we are exposing our children to in terms of our diet of the Bible, worship, prayer. New-borns are fascinated by faces and look at those talking to them. As new-borns in the kingdom we have to learn to spend time gazing at God to get to know him better. Ideas around contemplation and meditation have become slightly more well known as people take time to sit and gaze at God, within this practice the idea of soaking can easily be practiced with children (see the activities at the end of the chapter for how to do this). It also allows for what I call the 'sanctified imagination' to be engaged, an idea which arises from practices undertaken by contemplatives throughout church history of imagining with God.

> ## As new-borns in the kingdom we have to learn to spend time gazing at God to get to know him better.

Drawing and painting are also ways in which God can speak to and through children. Young children are usually less concerned about the accuracy or quality of the picture and are happy just to draw or paint. With many children the process of undertaking the painting is the important part, it is a journey or an expression and the finished product is less important. Children can use this type of mark making to express thoughts and emotions that they might not be able to put into words. A good friend of mine told me the following story of how God spoke to a child through a period of soaking and painting;

"I was doing a soaking session with a group of children. They had been lying on duvets and pillows and we'd been playing quiet music to them… Afterwards I gave them coloured pens and paper to draw or write what they'd seen or heard. One child aged about 7 picked up a handful of pens and holding them in one hand drew circles, round and round. I've learnt to watch not intervene…after the session finished and a few children had shared what happened for them, we released them. This child ran back into the room and said to me, " Did you see what I drew? Did you think I was just scribbling?" In the ensuing conversation she told me that she'd gone to heaven and found herself staring at a large throne. She had seen angels and she'd heard sounds vibrating in circles around the throne. When she listened, she could hear it was her name being spoken. She drew the picture to represent that. She asked me, does this make me special to God? I laughed and said "Yes." She replied "ok" and went out happy. Her parents had split up recently and she had been very distressed about this. I just loved seeing how her Heavenly Father had reached out to her. When our children connect with God themselves, it's so special. It has so much more impact than a parent or a friend reassuring them."

Not all children or adults may have this heavenly kind of experience, and we should not assume that because a child does that makes him or her something special. This little girl said that her mother has always listened to her and taken what she has said seriously but not made too much of it, it is just a part of her spiritual life and she finds it difficult if people think it is a 'special' gift. What we need to do is encourage all children to develop the relationship they do have and think about where we know they are in their walk with God and their understanding of the things of God.

Another early stage of communication development that we can draw on in thinking about how we learn to hear God is called 'joint attention'. It is when children and adults start paying attention to what each other is saying and doing, for example the parent follows the interest of the child and verbalises what the child is looking at, or the parent brings the attention of the child to an object by talking and pointing. In the same way God pays attention to us when we seek him, as James says if you *draw near to God ... he will draw near to you* (James 4:8). Our job then is to learn to follow what he is directing our attention to and acknowledge and respond to the gentle nudges of the Holy Spirit within. Helping children to identify the internal quiet prompts of the Holy Spirit through our careful listening to them and our attention on what is happening for them will help them grow in their encounters with God. We also need to be aware of the different ways in which God speaks as children may not hear him the same way we do, but we need to be open to helping them pursue what they hear.

Ways that God can communicate

God has created each one of us as unique and we have our own personalities and ways of being. God does not communicate to us all in exactly the same way. Often when he speaks it is internal and not like how we 'hear' other people, so we need to be clear when we are explaining this to children. The Bible shows that there are different ways in which God can speak and the next section explores many of these.

Scripture

The Bible as the word of God can be read in different ways and is always valuable to us (2 Timothy 3:16-17). At times the Holy Spirit will make some of the verses in scripture come alive to us and be specifically meaningful to us. This is the Rhema word (Greek meaning utterance) and is sometimes described as the now word of God. It is important for children to become familiar with scripture as this is one of the ways they get to know what God is like and how they can know whether what they are hearing is from him. Following a group activity where we had been looking at how God speaks to us through the scriptures, one 9 year old gave testimony the following week of how God had spoken to her through Ruth 1:16 *"Where you go I will go, and where you stay I will stay. Your people will be my people and your God my God,"* and how he told her that he would never leave her, that where she went he went and where she stayed he stayed. She found it really encouraging as there were some new uncertain things happening for her at the time.

Still small voice

It is most common for God to speak internally through what is often called the still small voice of God. Often the scripture used to illustrate this is Elijah in 1 Kings 19:12, which illustrates how God speaks in a whisper. This whisper is the internal voice of the Holy Spirit who lives within and he may speak in words or nudges or by bringing something or someone to mind. To ensure we are listening it helps to cultivate quiet on the inside of us by taking time just to be in God's presence. However, he can speak during our busy days by getting our attention through a sort of nudge or a word dropping into our mind or sometimes through a change in our feelings. When I was a new Christian God would often use the Spirit within me to bring my attention to some feelings I might be having. I would then ask him what they meant and sometimes it would be that I was feeling things for other people and he would want me to pray for them.

Pictures and visions

Pictures and visions are often internal pictures seen in the mind, they can be moving or still (Acts 10). Sometimes it can be that something seen in the natural vision becomes a prompt for God to say something in the spiritual realm (Jeremiah 1:11-12). Most pictures and visions need some interpretation and there is much more on how to interpret them in chapter 4.

Dreams

God can often speak in dreams because it is a time when our mind is less busy and there is less interference from all the day to day activity. John Paul Jackson called dreams night parables of God. This suggests they have a story-like element to them and they also need interpretation (see Daniel and Joseph as examples of interpreters of dreams). We can purposefully ask God to speak to us in our dreams as we pray at the end of the day. It is good practice to write down dreams when you wake so they are not forgotten. It is worth noting that God places a value on us having to figure things out with him and the Holy Spirit (Prov 25:2). Sometimes submitting a dream to others who have more experience in interpretation may be helpful.

Angels

It is important to think about angels as messengers of God because that is one of the functions they have in relation to men and women in the Bible; Luke 1 indicates angels speaking to Zechariah and Mary. However, this is such a large subject it will be covered in more detail in chapter 6.

The Audible voice of God

There are people who testify to hearing the audible voice of God, but even for them it is a rare occurrence and not the regular way in which we hear from God. What we can learn from the bible story of Samuel (1 Sam 3) is that the voice sounded ordinary and not spooky because Samuel thought it was Eli speaking to him.

Other people, circumstances and events

God can use anything to speak through, in one instance he even got a donkey talking (Numbers 22:28)! Commonly we might hear God through the prayer and counsel of friends, through prophetic words or through circumstances we live in.

Our personality, temperament, gender, culture, and experience may all affect the way we hear from God. We are unique individuals and God will use these characteristics in us to develop our relationship with him. He does not ask us all to be the same. God wants to speak to you for you. The key is whether we are actively listening or we are drifting in our day to day lives. Active listening implies making time to hear and asking him to speak. The parable of the sower in Matt 13:4 shows us how important it is that we respond effectively to the words God brings to us. His words are words of life and can transform us.

Activities for listening to God for ourselves.

The principle of all activities and activations where we are encouraging children to listen to God is that we take the first thing that we hear or that we see as God's word to us. We utilise what I think of as the sanctified imagination or the renewed mind (1 Cor 2:16). We do not need to spend a long time on these activities because often what will happen if we try to sit quietly for too long, is young children get bored and are more likely to make something up than listen to the first thing that enters their head. This may sound a simplistic approach but I believe and have experienced over the years that if we have asked God to speak to us we can trust him to do this. Employing feedback and teaching into activities helps us all to develop and grow as well. It is better to keep the activities simple to start with and not to spend too long on them but engage with them regularly. You will think of your own ways to do this as well. In the chapter on responding to God's words we will look at what we can do with these simple but powerful words that God gives us to help us develop the sense of God's identity in us.

1) Asking questions of God

One of the easiest ways to think about listening to God is to start by asking a question. To make this an appropriate and straightforward task I would suggest you ask questions that are going to promote God to speak into who we are. So we might just take a moment to be still and pray and then ask God how does he see us today? (This can be linked to the scripture of Gideon in the winepress if you want to combine with a teaching activity. Here God spoke to his identity and called him a mighty man of God in Judges 6)

It is typical that children might hear things such as they are kind, they are loving, they are helpful but they also might hear things like being generous or being an overcomer or being a light. Taking time to talk about what they hear is helpful as it provides an opportunity to unpack what might be a single word. For example what does it mean for a child to be an overcomer? Perhaps it relates to a situation God wants them to have confidence in, like school or some other area where they are finding things difficult. Linking the words God says to a specific situation will make them precise and more helpful on a day-to-day basis. It is always a good idea to ask them to ask the Holy Spirit for greater clarification of what might be an initial word or feeling, but if they do not hear anything it is okay for suggestions from you or others to help move forward. Practice at this will increase confidence and accuracy about not just how God sees them, but the application of that word for a specific situation. Then when they have a trouble or problem in life, they can use this simple activity as a practical aid to get them to change their view of the situation and see that God has equipped them for the time and the task.

One family who use this practice regularly shared an example of how when the child was getting anxious about something, she went to God and saw a picture of a white horse with a saddle and had the word pure. Her brother then pointed to a picture of a white horse in his Bible in Revelation, so they looked up the scripture. She also asked several others for their interpretation and was encouraged by the idea that God saw her as pure and the horse was for her to ride, lifting her above her anxieties.

2) The use of the sanctified imagination.

The principle of using sanctified imagination is based on the ancient tradition of Gospel contemplation promoted by St Ignatius of Loyola, where we invite God into our imaginations as we read the gospel and think about being in the scene. What I am proposing here is a first step for children into use of the imagination and can be used with even small children.

Get them to imagine that Jesus has come and sat by them. He wants to give them a game or something to play with, so together ask in a simple prayer that the Holy Spirit will show them what the game or activity is. Then get them to share these ideas. If you are doing this in church with a group of children, some of them may say the same as someone else. That does not matter as we remember this is an activation to help develop them, and children will be at different starting points not just in their knowledge and experience of God but also in their confidence and self-esteem. All these elements can make a difference to how children are able to engage. Children do naturally copy if they are unsure but will learn the more opportunity they have to practice.

The next step is to ask them to close their eyes again and get them to ask Jesus why he wants to give them this game or why he wants to play the game with them. For many the image they get will be of a familiar game or something they like to do and often they might feel that Jesus wants to play because he likes to spend time with them and he likes them to be happy. This is important for children to know, that spending time with Jesus actually brings him pleasure as well. However, some children may get some more complicated or profound insight into how God sees them and how he can work through them or use them. This may be age-related but also depends on how visual a child is and how much practice they have had in listening to God. One example I remember was where a child saw a chess set and felt God encouraging him that he had given him a strategic brain and he would use that in him.

The purpose of this activation is that it helps children move from receiving one idea (the game or activity), to going back and asking a second question and therefore encourages the start of a dialogue with the Holy Spirit. In encouraging them to develop the way they hear God and later the gift of prophecy we need to also show them that sometimes the first thing we see or hear is not all God wants to say. Practicing activities that encourage this kind of dialogue is very helpful.

3) Using Scriptures

It is vital that children get familiar with the scriptures so they can understand what God is like, what his nature is and how good he is. They can also see how the Holy Spirit can breathe on a portion of scripture and make it come alive to them. Take a few short portions of scripture (e.g. Psalm 28:7-9; Isaiah 43:1-7; Romans 8:14,16; Eph 1:3-6). Get the children to read them and then ask the Holy Spirit what he wants them to know from that scripture for themselves. To begin with their answers may be very short and may probably just repeat what the scripture says. However, you can develop this by asking questions related to life events that you know they are experiencing e.g. relationships with friends or siblings, things that are difficult at school, or emotions they are experiencing. Verses such as Col 2:6-7 *"So then, just as you received Christ Jesus as Lord, continue to live your lives in him, rooted and built up in him, strengthened in the faith as you were taught, and overflowing with thankfulness,"* could speak to them about a range of things. How God gives them strength for a situation, about Jesus being with them in a situation, about them growing in the faith and being more like him, about a way forward by finding things to be thankful for in a situation.

It is best not to presume what the Holy Spirit will say as his voice is very creative. During lockdown the children in our church were encouraged to use a memory verse each week and (re)present this to others through a picture, reading, song or other creative means. In one of those presentations, three children (aged 9 -11) had taken the verse in John 3:16 *"For God so loved the world that he gave his one and only Son, that whoever believes in him shall not perish but have eternal life"*. They explored what it meant to them and talked about how it reminded them of heaven. They said about how they used their imaginations and looked in the Bible for descriptions of heaven and then made a model of the golden heavenly city. This is a place where there are no tears, no death, no crying, no pain and the gate is always open. In the summary of the scripture they said we "have a promise that God will bring heaven to us and through us".

4) Soaking

Soaking is simply positioning ourselves in a place where we enter into the presence of God by the physical act of quieting our bodies and preparing to experience his love. Get children to make themselves comfortable on bean bags, or cushions and pillows on the floor. As they close their eyes, get them to take a few deep breaths in and out and then pray for the Holy Spirit to meet with them and show them something fresh. Put on some quiet music. It is natural for the mind to wander during this time, depending on the age of the child you can encourage them to refocus by gently offering some thoughts or scriptures during the period, or choosing music which has lyrics they can concentrate on.

When you sense they have had enough or some are getting distracted, bring the soaking time to a close with a prayer. At the end of the time get them to open up their eyes as they feel ready. You may want to chat about their experiences, or give them pens and paper to record them in some way. Soaking can be a deep encounter with God and they may not have words to express it, alternatively they may feel God gave them a picture or spoken to them clearly.

Chapter 3

PROPHECY AND WORDS OF KNOWLEDGE

"I would like every one of you to speak in tongues, **but I would rather have you prophesy.** *The one who prophesies is greater than the one who speaks in tongues, unless someone interprets, so that the church may be edified."* (I Cor 14:5)

Paul proposes that prophecy in the New Testament is available for all believers, *"you can all prophesy"* (1 Cor 14:31), and that it is a valuable gift for the believer because it builds up the church. He outlines foundations for the nature and purpose of prophecy in this passage by indicating the outcome these prophetic words should produce. *"But the one who prophesies speaks to people for their strengthening, encouraging and comfort (v3)"*, prophetic words are designed to build up, stir up and cheer up individuals, calling out who they are and the destiny God has placed within them. For many the prophetic word can act as a confirmation and encouragement of things God has already placed in their heart, or spoken to them about and it may (re)affirm their identity in God.

Inspirational words

This type of prophetic word is where every believer can start and can be considered as "forth telling"; speaking out the truths of God to an individual or group at a specific time that makes it relevant and powerful to them. It can be thought of as inspirational prophecy; rather than the traditional "foretelling" or revelatory prophecy which is better exemplified by the prophets in the Old Testament. In the Old Testament the prophet would be held to account for any word that did not come true, whereas what Paul is talking about is a gift that will encourage the body of Christ into their destiny in God.

Inspirational prophecy is often simple words, but given at the right time with the anointing of God. Recently one child told her mother she had heard the words "Heaven's gates are opening" in relation to another child. This other child had not been interested in church or anything to do with God for a while, but later said to her parents that she had been praying and found God was answering her prayers so she was ready to get to know Jesus. Obviously everyone was encouraged by the timing of the words.

> # Inspirational prophecy is often simple words, but given at the right time with the anointing of God.

Inspirational prophecy is a gift of the Spirit readily accessible for children to move in as it has clear boundaries with it aims to encourage others. There is no need for hype or the use of religious language, or phrasing like "God says" or "Thus says the Lord", rather individuals are able to share what they feel God is saying and there is room for feedback and growth. This type of prophetic word can be activated in all types of situations in church and outside of meetings. There is no need to wait for a prompting of the Holy Spirit to move in inspirational words, you can ask God what he wants to say to somebody when you see a need or if you just want to bless them e.g. on birthdays, or because they are having a difficult time, when they are starting something new like a job or school. There is one provision that needs to be noted which is that although prophecy may be personal for an individual, it is never private as something 'not to share' with others. All prophetic words should be opened up with someone else for accountability and possible help with interpretation and application.

The essence of moving in personal prophecy for others is built upon how individuals hear God for themselves. We move out of what we know of God, his character, his nature and his word. It should not be a strain to hear God for others if we have developed hearing him for ourselves. Living out a lifestyle of relationship with the Holy Spirit means we might find we are receiving daily prompts to action such as a nudge to pray for someone, or phone someone and then we find that our words or prayer occurred at just the right time. When I worked as manager of a nursery I was often in an office upstairs from the main nursery, but my nursery supervisor once said to me, "you always seem to arrive in the nursery when I need you". It was not something I was consciously aware of but clearly the internal nudge of the Holy Spirit was leading me about my daily work. Another friend remarked that I often contacted her at just the right time. Learning to respond to gentle nudges in our daily life helps us develop our relationship with the Holy Spirit, and a daily morning prayer for him to lead us that day to encourage others, opens up our spirits to his guidance.

It is important that we learn the ways God speaks to our children so that we can support their development and sometimes we need to use language that they can relate to and access. The idea of a sanctified or prophetic imagination may be easier for some children to access than the idea of hearing God or a still small voice. In our church we encourage everybody to share what first comes into their mind /imagination when we pray, believing that if we have asked God will speak. One of our children (age 8) who is part of our prophetic team explains how she hears God in her own words. "First he just gives me a picture of something like a light bulb and then I think who might this link to and I think it might link to a person called J and I can see that she has really good ideas and then God gives me something really encouraging about that, (for example) J's ideas can help people learn and then I've got my prophetic word". This is a helpful example of a sanctified imagination in practice.

The other thing to encourage is that individuals do not need to try and make their words long and involved. The key message is give only what you have from God, even if it only a little and resist the temptation or need to try and pad out with your own views or feelings. Very early on when I was starting to move in the prophetic someone gave me a word which said "don't worry if you only have a little thing to say", this really helped me to start moving out in the gift as sometimes we might only be given a word or a short phrase. It is also helpful therefore to pray for people with others, as someone else may have something to add to it. Including children in our prophetic appointments we have had to encourage this understanding in them, particularly as more experienced adults may have quite long words. However, evidence of maturity is shown when they are actually able to say "I don't have anything".

Worship often provokes an atmosphere where inspirational prophecy will flow, especially in a corporate setting. But it is important that we make time to worship all week if we want the gift to flow in us. The more we know of God the more we have to release and worship helps us focus on the truths of who he is. Worship also helps us to relax into who we are in God and so we do not need to strive but just commune with him. I also find that speaking in tongues helps to promote the flow of the Holy Spirit and can provoke my ability to hear God for others.

Creativity is also something that can be anointed by God and which can speak to us, in Exodus 31:1-11 men were chosen to help create the tabernacle and were anointed by God for the creative work they were to undertake. For us the creative may look different but it is not unusual to see dancers, flag bearers and painters as part of corporate worship. Similarly singers, songwriters and musicians can be anointed and storytellers and rappers can contribute God's words through their different giftings. One parent tells the following story; "my child of three was singing. I could hear them singing, "the angels bow down and worship you, they praise your name, they praise your name". I was shocked it was very clear sentences but I didn't know how he knew these things. It wasn't a worship song he had heard anywhere. I rushed to make notes in my journal as I knew he was hearing from God." We should not underestimate what God wants to do and will do through all of the church family. Sometimes we need to notice as this parent did, so that we can give due thanks and praise to God and so we can use the power of testimony to create more opportunities for God to move. Another child was doing some painting, she painted a peacock's feather and then found God speaking to her for an adult from the picture about the colour blue being linked to royalty.

Revelational words

When someone is confident in hearing God for inspirational words they may begin to receive more revelation. Revelation can include words of direction and destiny, they may also bring correction and challenge. However, all words still come from the heart of God's love for each one of us, so they should not bring condemnation. Revelation is about accessing something in heavenly realms and seeing something new. We have all had access to revelation at the moment when we realise that Jesus is Lord and Christ. The best example of this is in Matt 16:16-17 when Simon Peter says, *"You are the Messiah, the Son of the living God." Jesus replied, "Blessed are you, Simon son of Jonah, for this was not revealed to you by flesh and blood, but by my Father in heaven".* Similarly as believers we live in a revealed faith (John 16:13); *"when the Spirit of all truth comes, he will guide you into all the truth, for he will not speak on his own, but will speak whatever he hears, and will declare things to come".* Therefore, as the Holy Spirit now lives in us we receive revelation of the nature of God and Jesus.

This revelation can often be received and shared through teaching, reading the Bible, testimony and speaking, but can also be utilised in the prophetic. Revealed truth is powerful and changes us, as scripture says, *"you will know the truth and the truth will set you free"* (John 8:32). Paul indicates how the Holy Spirit reveals the deep things of God in 1 Cor 2:9-11;

> *as it is written:*
> *"What no eye has seen,*
> *what no ear has heard,*
> *and what no human mind has conceived" —*
> *the things God has prepared for those who love him—*
> *these are the things God has revealed to us by his Spirit.*
> *The Spirit searches all things, even the deep things of God.*
> *For who knows a person's thoughts except their own spirit within them? In the same way no one knows the thoughts of God except the Spirit of God.*

Utilising this understanding we can recognise that God will often show us something about himself that someone else may not have received a revelation of yet and it may help them in their current circumstance. There is still the requirement to ask the Holy Spirit how it applies, but the principle of sharing from our revelation a word from God can be powerful. One simple example that I have incorporated into words was when I 'saw' the principle in scripture that all seasons have a harvest of some kind at the end. I can now use this as a truth that can speak into any season someone is walking through. Other types of specific revelation for individuals may be more accurately classified as words of knowledge, this is when God gives you details about someone's life and circumstances that you did not know and these are discussed more fully below.

It is important that we also learn what to do with prophetic words when we receive them and this is discussed fully in Chapter 5, but as a starting point it is good practice to record all prophecies so that the process of weighing and judging can take place. Keeping a record of what God has said over the years is helpful in tracking God's actions in our lives and building faith. If the word is recorded on a phone, it's advisable to transcribe and have a written copy. If children are receiving words and their parents /carers are not there, they must be written down and shared with the responsible adults so there is openness and accountability.

Words of knowledge

There are diversities of gifts, but the same Spirit. There are differences of ministries, but the same Lord. And there are diversities of activities, but it is the same God who works all in all. But the manifestation of the Spirit is given to each one for the profit of all: for to one is given the word of wisdom through the Spirit, to another the word of knowledge through the same Spirit... (1 Corinthians 12:4-8).

Words of knowledge are a specific revelatory gift and can work in a number of ways, all of which are designed to build faith in the recipient (but often also encourage the one who gives them) by showing that God knows each person's situation. Words of knowledge help reveal God's supernatural nature and his lovingkindness for people. An accurate word often encourages greater faith in a believer or an openness in a non- believer to consider God.

> **Words of knowledge help reveal God's supernatural nature and his lovingkindness for people.**

Words of knowledge are often used in conjunction with the healing ministry in public forums, where an individual may receive a word of knowledge about another person's symptoms. The word when released then creates faith in the one who hears that God knows about them and wants to heal them and creates a platform for prayer. Sometimes a person is healed as the word is released without the need for prayer. Like the other gifts there is a need to grow and develop and recognise how God gives words of knowledge. Randy Clark teaches nine different ways that he has heard that people receive a word of knowledge for healing. There is some alignment in these with ways to hear God discussed in chapter 2, but there are also one or two additional ones itemised here. Individuals can feel something; this can be a pain in a part of the body momentarily and the knowledge it is not their pain, or they can feel an emotion like anxiety, fear or depression but know it is not their emotion. They get an impression from the Holy Spirit (think something), they see a body part or an injury, they are praying or speaking and say something they had not planned to say, they experience them, they dream them, they smell or taste something that is not there.

In the beginning of moving in this gift individuals should keep things simple and not over complicate what they have, or not assume if they receive two things that they are for the same person. There is a need to grow in discernment and a degree of trial and error with feedback is important. Small groups can be incubators and safe areas to practice all gifts of the Spirit. Some words of knowledge can be very specific with a lot of details. I remember once I had a word of knowledge for someone about a back/neck injury caused by falling off a horse about 20 years ago and although no one responded straight away, someone came up to me after the meeting who had never seen words of knowledge in action before. He wanted to know how I knew about what had happened to him as he had had a bad injury as a child that still caused difficulties and it was wonderful to pray with him and explain God's love for him through the word.

Words of knowledge can also be used in evangelism, through activities like Christian treasure hunting which utilises the practice of God showing ahead of time things that would be found when those praying are out talking to people. For example individuals may have received pictures of items of clothing, colour of hair or eyes, items that are being carried which are then written on a piece of paper. When they are out and about and see these they can then approach the person and introduce themselves by saying that God has shown them these things because he wants to tell them how much he cares about them. Words of knowledge for healing of unbelievers are very powerful as they can introduce people to the reality of God. Only today I heard a testimony from a friend who got a word of knowledge about a bad right knee as he was walking up the street and saw someone he knew from his neighbourhood. He was able to share, pray and see the knee heeled, because he paid attention to the word God dropped into his mind.

Words of knowledge may also be the first step in receiving a significant prophetic word for an individual. However, sometimes these need to be handled with wisdom. What we initially receive through the word of knowledge may be diagnostic, with God simply informing us about the situation, content and background of where the individual is. He will not want us to prophesy the problem, they already know the difficulties they are facing. At this point we need to take a step back and ask God what his solution is for the problem or challenge they face and that is what we prophesy. If we only stop with the diagnosis we are not helping them see that God is providing a way through. As a feeler I can sometimes sense what others may be carrying emotionally, but I know this is God getting my attention, not what he wants me to speak out. Sometimes if I get nothing more I realise the word of knowledge is just a call for me to pray into that situation.

Activities for developing prophetic words.

All activities we used in the chapter on listening to God for ourselves can be adapted to hearing God for others. The important fact is that we are intentional in asking God to speak through us and we use the measure of faith that we have. Similarly all these activities may be used to invite the Holy Spirit to talk to us personally.

1) Using pictures - prophetic imagination

As discussed earlier one of the ways in which God can speak to us is through pictures or visions. To activate this all you need are some pictures, which can be gathered from birthday cards, photographs and magazines. Choose someone who you are going to prophesy over and get them to choose a picture that appeals to them, alternatively you can put the pictures face down and they can choose randomly. I have undertaken this activity with small groups of children and adults and always found they engage and start hearing God. I always try and demonstrate one example so they understand what the principles of the activity are before they get involved.

Pray before you start that the Holy Spirit will speak as you look at the picture. To begin with you may just see what is obvious but it is important to then ask the Holy Spirit what that means for the person you are praying for. Everyone might see something different or sometimes several people will see the same thing but have a slightly different interpretation. If this activity is taking place in a group it is likely contributions will build from one another as often there is a sense of a general witness to things which are from the Spirit of God. It is always useful to check at the end whether what has been said means something to the person receiving the word and whether they have been encouraged by it. This also provides encouragement to those prophesying and is helpful in the growth of individuals. It is helpful for the children to be able to keep the picture as it provides a visual reminder of the words that God has spoken to them and God may keep speaking to them through it as well.

I was doing a workshop recently with some boys and one was missing so his friends decided they would like to send something to him. They chose a picture of a beach with some cliffs. These are some of the things they and their parents felt God say through the picture;

"People on the cliffs have a good view of everything that is going on and can help others stay safe. You will be someone who can see into the distance, and can watch out for others in trouble.

God loves your heart which is soft and warm, and like the sand he is able to shape you and make you into what he wants.

As the sea shapes the pebbles and stones on the beach, God will do the same for you. As God and his Holy Spirit wash over you he will make you more like him. As the waves wash over the pebbles it's like a blessing from God. You will be taught new things as God washes over you.

You will face obstacles and challenges in life, but you will get through them because Jesus is with you and with him you will find excitement and fun in the adventure and the challenges just like swimming in the sea".

Sometimes children may see something but not be able to clearly articulate the meaning. As an example one day we were utilising this activation with a group of children aged 7 to 12. The picture that was chosen was of some grains or seeds. One of the eight year olds made a link to the story of Joseph and the dream of the sheaves of corn. They did not have the experience or the wisdom to know how to apply that to the girl who it was for. As the adult who was leading the session I was able to support with the interpretation that God would speak to her through dreams. We checked with the parent and the girl herself that she did indeed often dream. It was possible to encourage her to believe that dreams were from God and to write them down in future and share them with her parents. This became a helpful learning opportunity for everyone.

It may be that it is not the picture itself that sparks something in the prophetic imagination; but simply a colour of the picture, or a reminder for an individual of another time or place. This is perfectly acceptable as all the picture is being used for is the starting point to ask God to speak. When God spoke to Jeremiah about the almond tree he not only gave a message but used wordplay to get the message across, demonstrating a familiar cultural technique of the day. We should be open therefore to receiving different ways of seeing the same thing.

It is possible to undertake this activity with children in church who may not have given their lives to Jesus, they can still hear him speak to them and I believe undertaking this type of encounter where they ask God to speak opens them up to God's love for them. It is also possible to use pictures as a way of delivering God's message to those who do not yet know him ensuring that the language used is not religious but accessible to all.

Practicing hearing God like this might also help those children who hear from God in pictures. Just recently a parent of a five you old shared with me that her son had just come into her and said he had seen a picture of two open hands holding another child. He said they were God's hands and God loved him a lot. This is a child who had not previously been interested in talking about things about God, but who then explained that God had given him lots of pictures.

2) The gift - utilising questions.

In all my years of undertaking these types of activations one of the things I have learnt is that it is very easy to get a picture, to get an idea or to get the starting point of a prophetic word. Often people stop there and this can lead to a lack of clarity in what is given and received. This activation is designed to help move into the next step of hearing God more deeply through using questions.

Working in small groups (3 or 4 people) everyone chooses one person to receive the prophetic word. After a short prayer asking the Holy Spirit to reveal himself through the words, ask God what kind of gift he would like to give that person. This gift can be something physical and tangible like a balloon or it can be something more intangible like peace, joy, and love. When everybody has received the first step of what the gift is, you then pray again and this time ask the questions why does God want them to have this gift? And what is it going to help them be or do? In one instance a child had a picture for an adult of a hair clip and went on to say she thought it was because it was designed to keep the hair out of her eyes so that she could see more clearly what God was doing at this time and would be less distracted and worried by what was in front of her eyes. Another instance I remember is of a child who saw a present of a hamster ball, and felt that God was saying he wanted to use the child to help those who thought they were free (like the hamster) but were really still in a cage. In both these examples the actual picture (present) is less important than what God wants to say from it.

As in the previous chapter on hearing God for ourselves the

creation of a dialogue with the Holy Spirit helps to focus and provide a context for a very general word. Developing prophetic ministry is about taking encouraging words and seeing them become more specific and relevant for the person who is receiving them. Asking questions helps to focus on what else God might be staying beyond what we first receive.

As an alternative to this activity, you can use real objects; for example our homegroup always does a prophetic gift at Christmas. Here we wrap a small gift which can often be something regifted, home made or from a charity shop. They are then put in a bag and randomly given out to everyone. Then as a group we prophecy for each person as they open the gifts. It is amazing how often the gift itself matches the individual as well as the words that come from it.

3) **Using scripture**

Using scripture as a starting point for prophecy is very common but often I have experienced someone just giving me the scripture with no explanation. While this may be encouraging it is not as powerful as finding out more of what is in God's heart for someone. The principle of asking questions applies here as well. Why does God want them to have that scripture? What part of that scripture is most specific to their situation? What area of their life might God be talking into? This activity is probably the best with slightly older children who know some of the Bible and who can write clearly. It can be completed as a staged approach where they start with the scripture and then ask each question in turn. Once all the answers are written down they can be crafted into a word. Here is a generic example from Psalm 139 that we used to encourage individuals inside cards. It speaks truth without necessarily being specific for a single person.

> I see you and I know you. I LOVE you. I know your mind and your heart, and I understand you even as you've grown and evolved. It's been a remarkable process. I've always known you - even when you kicked inside of your mother. In the

world, you may sometimes feel invisible or insignificant, but you are beautiful and wondrous to me. There's no one like you. I know the future looks uncertain, but it is my joy to protect your today and your tomorrow - so don't worry. I think about you all the time, and I have good things in store for you. Your life is important to me, and nothing you do can make me go away. I am here for you and I give you a constant supply of strength and guidance. (Psalm 139)

Another way to approach it is to choose some short passages of scripture about 3-4 verses long, then identify an individual who the passage is for and ask the children to see which word or phrase from the passage is highlighted to them as it is read. To do this read the verses a couple of times out loud and then give those praying a chance to ask the Holy Spirit why that word or phrase might be important for someone. Here is an example where we also used Psalm 139 verses 1-5 with a group of girls and their mums for a friend of theirs;

God is with you however far you go.
There is no set place that makes you close to God.
He is with you all the time, wherever you are.

Whatever you are doing, He's there to help you,
He is close to you, even if you go to different places and do different things to others.
He knows you (name) and knows what you love, he loves those things too.
He knows you intimately,
He loves how he has made you.

God knows everything there is to know about you (name)
He knows every joy and pain, He understands you.
He knows the secrets of your heart and wants to take from you the things that upset you.

In the times where you feel wobbly, or like you have different interests or passions.

When you are worried or don't feel your normal bubbly self,
He is with you and knows how to help.

He loves knowing you, you bring Him such joy and delight,
He understands you,
He loves you,
He values you,
He sees you in the secret place.

Another way of using scriptures is when God brings to mind a particular Bible character. Again apply the principle of asking the Holy Spirit questions. Why is this character important? What aspects of the character and their relationship with God does this person have that are relevant for now and why might God be saying this at this time?

For many years God would give me words for young men from some of David's mighty men (2 Sam 23:8-39). These were identity and destiny words. It is worth remembering that just because you have given a word to someone it does not negate God speaking something similar again for a different person, but it may perhaps have a different emphasis.

Practicing words of knowledge

This is usually more of a corporate activity but can happen as part of preparation for worship or during worship. It is always helpful in a corporate setting to remind people how God gives words of knowledge and then invite them to share these; perhaps by writing on post it notes or a board in a face to face meeting, or as we did recently utilising the chat feature in a zoom service. People then responded to the words and were prayed for by those who had given them.

Chapter 4

SPEAKING IN TONGUES, DREAMS AND INTERPRETATION

I remember after I was filled with the Holy Spirit I wanted to speak in tongues, so I opened my mouth and expected something to come out and nothing happened. It was only when God told me I had to speak that I actually made a sound and it took awhile for me to become fluent in the language that I was given. Speaking in tongues (other languages) is a gift of the Holy Spirit that was given to the disciples at Pentecost when the Holy Spirit was poured out. This is illustrated in the account in Acts 2:4 *"All of them were filled with the Holy Spirit and began to speak in other tongues as the Spirit enabled them"*.

Many of us may not have had the same dynamic experience as these early disciples and can therefore feel or conclude tongues is not for us, especially as it remains a controversial topic in some parts of the church. I want to explore in this chapter why speaking in tongues is important based on Pauls' teaching in 1 Cor 14, how the gift can be used to build ourselves in God as individuals and contribute to building up the church and how we can encourage its everyday use in our lives.

That first great outpouring of the Spirit in Acts 2 goes on to explain how,

> *a crowd came together in bewilderment, because each one heard their own language being spoken. Utterly amazed, they*

asked: "Aren't all these who are speaking Galileans? Then how is it that each of us hears them in our native language? Parthians, Medes and Elamites; residents of Mesopotamia, Judea and Cappadocia, Pontus and Asia, Phrygia and Pamphylia, Egypt and the parts of Libya near Cyrene; visitors from Rome (both Jews and converts to Judaism); Cretans and Arabs—we hear them declaring the wonders of God in our own tongues!" Amazed and perplexed, they asked one another, "What does this mean?"

This passage makes it clear that the result of the outpouring of the Holy Spirit on this occasion caused the disciples to magnify and praise God. The disciples were speaking known languages, even though they may not have understood what they were saying. I have heard testimonies of this happening, someone speaking a public tongue in church is asked afterwards where they learnt the language, and also accounts of people being able to speak in a whole new language so they can act as interpreters or missionaries. However, for most of us, we start small and grow and tongues are used for our own development and relationship with God.

From Acts 2 we have seen that God gives us real languages to speak, although Paul notes that these may be languages of the angels and well as human languages (1 Cor 13:1). A language will have structure, syntax and intonation, everything in fact that any language contains. However, when we are first learning to speak in tongues we may only have a few words to start with and we may seem to babble like babies do when they are learning to talk. It is important to know that the one speaking in tongues has control over what they say, they are not taken over by sounds coming out of their mouth. Nowhere in the Bible does it suggest that speaking in tongues is an ecstatic state where people lose control or lose sense of their surroundings. The one speaking in tongues can start and stop at their will.

If we need to be built up in God we should make tongues a part of our regular devotions.

I believe we need to encourage speaking in tongues as an important gift of the Holy Spirit and clear teaching and modelling of tongues and their benefit is essential. Paul says in I Cor 14:1-5 that tongues are useful for edifying ourselves, so if we need to be built up in God we should make tongues a part of our regular devotions.

Prayer Language (The Message)

Go after a life of love as if your life depended on it—because it does. Give yourselves to the gifts God gives you. Most of all, try to proclaim his truth. If you praise him in the private language of tongues, God understands you but no one else does, for you are sharing intimacies just between you and him...The one who prays using a private "prayer language" certainly gets a lot out of it, but proclaiming God's truth to the church in its common language brings the whole church into growth and strength. I want all of you to develop intimacies with God in prayer, but please don't stop with that.

Just as parents delight over their children's first few words, I'm sure our Heavenly Father delights in us as we trust him and use the gift he gives us. Using the words we have been given over and over again is fine, after all we often repeat phrases such as Praise God or Hallelujah, but we should expect new words to come and for there to be a greater fluency the more the gift is utilised. It is possible that over a period of time this prayer language of tongues that you have been given may change and you may find you are speaking in another language. I have particularly found this happen when I am in intercession or sometimes if I give a public tongue.

I like to explain why I use tongues in several ways. It is clear from the passage in 1 Cor 14 that tongues is prayer or worship directed to God, *"For anyone who speaks in a tongue does not speak to people but to God. Indeed, no one understands them; they utter mysteries by the Spirit"* *(1 Cor 14:2)*. Sometimes when I'm praying and worshipping I run out of words to tell God how wonderful I think he is. Although I might start in English I can then continue in tongues, knowing that I am praising and declaring just how great he is, as the disciples in Acts 2 did. This can either be in spoken prayer, but also through singing in the Spirit. Another time when it is really helpful to use tongues as a form of prayer is when I am praying for a situation that is so big that I do not really know how to pray. I just know God is the answer. Romans 8:26-27 tells us that the Spirit can pray through us in wordless groans and intercedes for us, but equally he can use tongues to give words to our intercession.

These examples are ways of explaining when tongues might be used in a personal way, however in order to encourage others to use the gift of tongues they need to be demonstrated by those who are fluent. So I would encourage everyone to make it part of prayer and worship times both at home and in the small and larger congregational meetings, and as Paul says *"I would like every one of you to speak in tongues"* (1 Cor 14:5) it needs to be made clear that it is a gift to be desired and used.

If we read the passages in the Acts of the apostles on speaking in tongues (Acts 2, 10 and 19), it appears to be a sign that disciples had received the baptism in the Spirit when they spoke in tongues. Historically there has been teaching in the church to suggest that if you did not speak in tongues you were not filled with the Spirit. In Acts 10:44-45 however there was something else happening as these were gentile believers receiving the Holy Spirit for the first time. It was important that their experience matched those of the Jewish believers to show how the gift of faith in God through Jesus was now available for all mankind.

While Peter was still speaking these words, the Holy Spirit came on all who heard the message. The circumcised believers who had come with Peter were astonished that the gift of the Holy Spirit had been poured out even on Gentiles. For they heard them speaking in tongues and praising God (Acts 10:45-46).

There are also many verses in Acts of incidents where believers were filled with the Spirit that do not mention tongues (2:37-42; 8:26-40; 9:1-19; 13:44-52; 16:11-15; 16:25-34; 17:1-10a; 17:10b-15; 17:16-33; 18:1-11; 18:24-28). But this does not mean we should not encourage Spirit filled believers to ask for the gift, just that we should not take it as a sign of a person being Spirit filled.

Paul talks about how when we are speaking in tongues it is the Spirit speaking but the mind is unfruitful. *"For if I pray in a tongue, my spirit prays, but my mind is unfruitful"* (1 Cor 14:14). Some people may use this as an argument for not speaking in tongues, however as we have already seen, praying, praising, and giving thanks in tongues is deemed to edify the individual even if it bypasses the mind. I often used to pray in tongues on the journey down the motorway to work. I needed my mind to be focused on the driving, but my spirit was free to worship God and praising God in this way prepared me spiritually for the day. Perhaps the greatest argument for praying in tongues as part of our private devotions is that Paul said *"I thank God that I speak in tongues more than all of you"* (1 Cor 14:18). Paul was a rational, highly educated man who accomplished great deeds for the kingdom, but who also suffered for it, *"I have worked much harder, been in prison more frequently, been flogged more severely, and been exposed to death again and again."* (2 Cor 11:23). Perhaps building up his spirit with speaking in tongues was part of the arsenal he had to enable him to endure and persevere through these trials, if so, we would certainly benefit from using tongues regularly in our devotions.

A gift of tongues and interpretation

Occasionally a member of a congregation will be inspired to give a public tongue, this is when they speak in tongues usually from the front of a meeting for everyone to hear. The guidance from Paul is clear that in a public meeting there must be an interpretation and that no one should give a tongue unless they are prepared to interpret. *"For this reason the one who speaks in a tongue should pray that they may interpret what they say"* (1 Cor 14:13). The Greek word for interpret (diermeneuo) signifies to interpret fully, to explain or unfold the meaning. It is the same word used of Jesus interpreting the scriptures to the disciples on the road to Emmaus (Luke 24:13-35). This is not therefore the sense of a word for word translation of a tongue but something that might also carry an explanation of the meaning behind the tongue.

1 Cor 14:2 says that *"anyone who speaks in a tongue does not speak to people but to God. Indeed, no one understands them; they utter mysteries by the Spirit"*, suggesting that tongues are directed towards God. Therefore, when we are thinking about an interpretation of a public tongue it is possible that it will be something that praises and lifts up the majesty of who God is and his relationship with us. In my experience what also appears to happen once a tongue is given is that the use of one gift of the Spirit starts the release of another and prophetic words often follow when people are giving interpretations. Paul is clear that prophecy is superior to tongues in a public setting (1 Cor 14:19), so that people understand what is being said, so if one leads to the other that is a positive experience for everyone present.

Dreams

Dreams are one of the ways God can speak to us and it is clear from scripture that he will use dreams and visions to communicate with us (Numbers 12:6, Hos 12:10) *"I will pour out of My Spirit upon all flesh: and your sons and your daughters shall prophesy, and your young men shall see visions, and your old men shall dream dreams"* (Acts 2:17). If we look at biblical examples we can also see he does not restrict speaking through dreams to just to those who know him. In Joseph's life he interpreted dreams for at least three people who were not followers of the One True God (Genesis 39 and 41). We can also see in the Bible how God spoke to those who knew him in dreams, the Christmas story provides the example of Joseph (Matt 2:12-13).

Dreams can be very powerful times of communication and counsel from God (Ps. 16:7), and scripture shows us that God does significant things within dreams. For example, he established the Abrahamic Covenant in a dream (Gen 15:12,13,18) and God granted supernatural gifts through dreams (I Kings 3:5,9,12,15). It is important to take our dreams seriously and use them wisely as part of the spiritual gifts given to us. Although we all dream, there are some people for whom this is one of the most powerful and regular ways that God speaks and there is a need to become consistent in writing dreams down and then seeking their interpretation. Even for those of us who do not regularly receive dreams, we can ask God to speak to us this way in order to develop and grow.

As a practical point many children may have a stage in life where they have bad dreams or night terrors but this does not mean they are encountering the demonic. Often with night terrors this is a development stage (between 3-8 years old) that some children go through and they do not usually remember them in the morning. Nightmares or bad dreams occur most commonly between the ages of 3-6 and can be caused by worry and stress or watching something scary before bedtime. A good relaxing bedtime routine which includes prayer before sleep is helpful. As parents we take responsibility for the atmosphere in our homes and need to be calm and matter of fact when dealing with children's fears helping them to find peace and calm through our responses to events that occur for them.

What is generally true about most dreams is that we will not necessarily understand the meaning without some further conversation with the Holy Spirit, both for the interpretation, but also the application of the dream. Unlike the inspirational gift of prophecy dreams may contain direction and warnings as well as encouragement. Wisdom is essential in helping children to work through what they are receiving in their dreams. There are many resources that suggest that dream interpretation is about knowing that there are symbols that have meanings (see section on symbolism below). This is applicable as a starting point but we must remember that the Bible clearly shows that interpretation is also a gift of the Holy Spirit (as in the examples of Joseph and Daniel). It is important therefore not to apply a hard and fast code to interpretation. It takes practice to develop skills in this area.

Generally a dream will be interpreted on a personal level unless there is a clear guidance of the Holy Spirit that it is for someone else. In a dream you may have been watching something happen or you may have been a character with things happening to you, it is important to ask why this may be and think about what this might mean. Identifying the main themes, circumstances and emotional context can help to organise the dream interpretation and keeping it simple helps build the interpretation. In Zechariah 4 we can see how in his dream he did not pretend to know things, but was open to being told by the heavenly messenger the meaning of what he was seeing. Contemplating the dream in reference to the Holy Spirit, persevering in the process of interpretation and searching the scriptures are all part of the process of dream interpretation. Opening the dream up to others for their input and help is a way of ensuring accountability and remaining in relationship just as we do for prophetic words.

One child has often had dreams of heaven where she has dreamt of parties and rooms being prepared. Once she dreamed about a special chess set being laid out in heaven in a room with the name of an elderly member of her congregation on. When he passed away a week or so later the dream gave a lot of joy and comfort to those left behind, because their father had been a chess champion when younger, but not played in recent years so it was unlikely this child could have had prior knowledge of this.

Principles of interpretation for all spiritual gifts

Many of the ways God speaks to and through us benefit from interpretation, although tongues is the only gift that requires one when given publicly, because it is clearly in a language we can not understand. God speaks in symbols and pictures, and through dreams, visions and prophecy. Take for example Peter's vision in Acts 10:12-17

> *He saw heaven opened and something like a large sheet being let down to earth by its four corners. It contained all kinds of four-footed animals, as well as reptiles and birds. Then a voice told him, "Get up, Peter. Kill and eat."*
>
> *"Surely not, Lord!" Peter replied. "I have never eaten anything impure or unclean."*

In this story Peter doesn't actually understand the meaning of the picture straight away, twice it talks about him thinking about its meaning... *"while Peter was wondering about the meaning of the vision"* (v17 and 19). It is only as we read the story of what follows that we realise Peter has equated the vision and God's command with this opportunity to minister to gentiles, those who were thought by the Jews to be impure and unclean (Acts 10:28).

Interpretations of tongues and of visions and dreams are not opinions, but a gift of the Holy Spirit. There are some principles of interpretation that apply to all gifts and understanding the language of the Bible and the ways of God, helps in providing interpretations. The Bible is full of figurative language and Jesus himself spoke in parables because God places value on us having to figure things out (Proverbs 25:2). Moreover, having to rely on the Holy Spirit and others in the body to help with the interpretation means we rely on God in dependence and others in interdependence, key elements of the relationships we are building together.

> # Interpretations of tongues and of visions and dreams are not opinions, but a gift of the Holy Spirit.

Symbolism

The Bible is full of symbolism and many have interpreted the meanings of images and symbols from scriptures and we can learn from their experience. Symbols are generally regarded as typifying or representing something else e.g. the cross is seen throughout the world as a symbol for Christianity. But symbols can have layers of meaning e.g. the phrase 'Lamb of God' can infer sacrifice, Jesus' gentleness, God the protector, the passover, obedience and submission, as well as the lamb of Isaiah 53. But even when there is a degree of familiarity with symbols it is important to rely on the Holy Spirit because symbols can represent different things to different people at different times.

A few of the common symbols from the Bible and their meanings are:-

Sheep – which can indicate the people of God; or qualities such as innocence, vulnerability; humility; or actions such as submission; sacrifice.

Numbers – where there is some agreement based on how they are used in scripture e.g. the number 5 often represents grace, the number 7 perfection or completion. This is because when they are used in scripture they always have the same meaning.

Colours – Blue in the Bible for example, means the heavens or the word of God. It is sometimes translated as purple or violet and was the colour associated with priests clothing. Purple is also associated with royalty and majesty.

But it should be remembered that the interpretation may also be related to the context in which the symbol is seen for example the meaning of colours could be either positive or negative depending on how they were portrayed in the dream or vision.

As with all prophetic interpretation, we need to consider that we are individuals with our own history with God and sometimes words, phrases or pictures have a depth of meaning for us they would not have for others. For example, I once had a dream involving some friends where I saw a big black dog running up and down the boundary of their property. I shared it with a good friend who is practiced at dream interpretation and we decided the dream was a call to prayer for me as I do not often have such clear and vivid dreams. It was a warning of a spiritual attack that was hovering around them as the dog, to me, was threatening and black in colour and this later proved to be a correct interpretation. However, to someone else who likes dogs it could easily have had a different meaning. Similarly in the Bible both Jesus and Satan are described as lions. Jesus is the Lion of Judah in Rev 5:5 and Satan is described as prowling like a devouring lion (1 Peter 5:8). However, we can be confident that God will make his purposes clear to us if we follow him and rely on him, as we are informed that we have the mind of Christ (1 Cor 2:16).

Two examples from scripture that encourage us to rely not just on what we know but the revelation from the Holy Spirit are in the stories of Joseph and Daniel who are both known for interpreting dreams. Joseph declares that interpretations belong to God and that it is God who will give Pharaoh his answer (Gen 40:8 and 41:15) and in the book of Daniel (2:16-19) we see how he took the route of humility and dependence by asking his friends to help pray with him for the interpretation. Knowing God is the single most important element in interpreting tongues, dreams, vision, and revelation. We need to understand God's nature and character and the way in which he works. We also need to understand his timing. God may be speaking for now, for the future, or confirming something he has already said.

Activities to facilitate tongues and interpretation

How to speak in tongues – getting started

One way of beginning to speak in tongues requires a corporate experience, where following a prayer for the Holy Spirit to be present and fill everyone, everybody who can use the gift just starts praying in tongues for a little while (2 or 3 minutes and loud enough so that others can have a go without feeling obvious). The children can be encouraged to listen and they can join in by copying or imitating what they hear. This is not that different from how any language might be learnt through copying and repeating the sounds or repeating the phrases. It is also helpful because it gets the idea that you have to make a sound or noise, the tongue does not just come automatically out of an open mouth. Those who start speaking in tongues in this way can then be encouraged to continue in their personal times with God. Equally this can happen at home during prayer where those who can use the gift do so regularly and naturally.

For some singing in tongues may be easier than speaking and then what you could do is just put on some worship music and as you start to sing think about praising God in a new language and about creating a new song that is yours. Other people have indicated that sometimes it is easier to speak in tongues when doing something else, for example in the shower as you cannot hear yourself so loudly and therefore it may seem less embarrassing to begin with.

Activities for Interpretation.

Interpreting tongues.

Paul encourages us to practice the gift of interpretation when we speak in tongues. So we can practice both speaking in tongues and interpretation at the same time. Or we can get someone who is confident to speak in a tongue and then we can have a go at interpreting. Remember the rules of who God is and how he speaks will apply. Interpretations should either be directed towards praising God or should encourage and build up those who hear them.

To continue developing interpretation it is good to occasionally ask God, as you pray in tongues, what the interpretation is, this way you are using both your spirit and your mind when praying (1 Cor 14:13-14).

Interpreting pictures and objects

See the activity in Chapter 3 on giving prophecies using pictures as the starting point for thinking about interpretation. As much of what we receive from God in pictures, visions and dreams is visual, practicing interpreting from pictures and objects helps us develop our ability to hear God.

Utilising symbols.

This activation uses some symbols that represent God's nature in the Bible e.g. fire, water, wine, oil, and bread, to help think about how they speak to us in our lives.

For children it is possible to start with pictures of each of the symbols.

First pray and ask which symbol they feel God wants to speak through for a specific person. Then ask what aspect of God's character they feel is represented by that symbol for the person they are praying for.

For example you might feel that God gives the symbol fire. In the Bible fire has several different applications: it is typical of a theophany indicating the presence of God but can also be used as a symbol of refining and purifying, it is also related to consuming (a sacrifice), or testing, and as a symbol of the Holy Spirit coming in power and revival. It also has meanings in the natural related to food and warmth as a contained fire, but causes damage as a wildfire. So utilising the question and answer approach with the Holy Spirit it is important to find out which of these meanings the symbol represents on this particular occasion for this particular person.

Obviously when doing this as a group it is highly likely that children may hear different aspects, especially when we are introducing this to them, some of the aspects they are most familiar with may have more resonance. However, by getting feedback from the person who they have chosen the symbol for about the accuracy or relevance of each of the aspects chosen we can help develop our skills. As with all activations we are not expecting to get everything 100% accurate the first time.

Chapter 5

RESPONDING TO GOD'S WORDS

Very early in my Christian life God gave me a word from an empty picture frame. The word was that he wanted to put his picture of me into my heart and that was why the frame was empty. It was many years later I had another empty picture frame as a gift and this time I heard him say. "You now have my picture of you in your heart". I am so thankful for God's kindness along my journey to accepting my identity and giving me the second word, especially as the process to accepting who I am, had been a bumpy ride. But what I learnt through the process was that God is always more interested in who we are than in what we are able to do. In Exodus 3:3 God defined himself by his own existence *"I am who I say I am"* and as we are made in the image of God (Gen 1:27) understanding our identity often involves understanding how we are like God.

However, as well as speaking into our identity God is going to speak about our destiny and calling and I discovered that giving or receiving a prophetic word is only half the story, we also have a responsibility to walk with God to see the word outworked and that some words may take a long time to be fulfilled. We are required to cooperate with the Holy Spirit in the process, not try to fulfil the words ourselves (look at what happened when Abraham tried to fulfil his word and Ishmael was born). We need therefore to bear in mind that all prophecy is conditional and there are things we may need to do to see fulfilment.

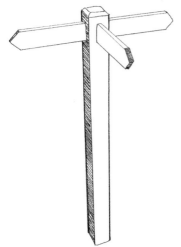

Often the conditions in a word are not explicit, for example destiny and future calling words are often signposts to what is in God's heart. The wise counsel of others and the Holy Spirit help us to see what steps might need to be taken to walk into that destiny. A call to be an evangelist may not mean you are going to be the next Billy Graham with a worldwide ministry, you have to work with God to establish the area he is calling you into now (it could be a school, college, university, club, workplace or neighbourhood for example). It may mean preparing by ensuring you have a clear testimony to share or you might need to volunteer for an Alpha or find a mentor who is already moving in the gift. My husband and I have a lot of words over our life about being parents in the church, so we decided when we came to move house that we needed to place ourselves in the physical locality of where the young families were that we might be called to share life with. The house also needed to be suitable to host families for meals and shared times together, this required us investing in an extension. However, this was a way of us preparing and working with what God had said so that we positioned ourselves for the fulfilment of the word.

Prophetic words are only part of the process of what God is saying and doing in someone's life and rarely standalone. We prophesy in part (1 Cor 13:9), and our word may be part of a series the other person is receiving over time. Scripture is clear that words need to be weighed and judged (1 Cor 14:29) and 1 Thess 5:19-21, encourages us to *"not despise prophetic utterances, but examine everything carefully and hold fast to what is good"*.

Our response needs to indicate that we are valuing what God gives us through prophetic words. Prophecy can be despised in a variety of ways and we should note when we have a negative reaction to something that is being given and examine ourselves, it may be that God wants to provoke an attitude change in us! We may give lesser attention or value to a word if we do not like something that is said or perhaps we do not value the giver (e.g. do I listen to children in the same way as experienced adults?), or perhaps we react to the way it is said (e.g. with too much enthusiasm or too much spiritual language). If we do not receive the word at the beginning with a heart of faith we are in danger of despising it. Some of the significant encouraging words I have received have been simple statements from children and young people, but given at exactly the right time in response to something I have prayed. Another example was a word my husband received in church from two children that others were wary of because it talked about sin and forgiveness, however to him it was a confirmation of his pursuit of holiness.

Examining God's words

There are some simple procedures that can be applied to confirm if the word we receive is from God. The starting point is that the prophetic word should bring freedom, any word that carries negativism and judgmentalism is not from the heart of the God who loves us so extravagantly. Because God is not motivated by judgment but love for humankind, even if he is encouraging somebody to repent or change things, he will say it in a way that can be received and not condemn anyone.

God's word may convict but will never condemn.

Here are some ways we can examine (weigh and judge) prophetic words: -

1) Ask does the word comply with the spirit of the Bible.

Scripture provides principles and practice of how God works and reveals his nature and character. As all prophetic words flow out of the heart of God we can line it up with the principles of scripture and in particular the life of Jesus, who is the word of God. His voice through the prophetic will not contradict his written word. This is one of the reasons why it is so important to engender a love for the Bible when pursuing growth in any prophetic gifting.

2) The essential flavour of the word should draw people closer to God. It must not cause confusion, condemnation or discouragement as God is a God of order not chaos. Any individuals who have had poor experiences with prophetic words that have shut them into a corner may need healing prayer and release from these.

3) The inner witness of the Holy Spirit is vital in receiving a word. We must have confidence in the Holy Spirit to lead us into truth both when we give and when we receive a word. Sometimes there are words that do not settle in the heart immediately and it may be important that we give them time and ponder them with God (Luke 2:19). Once I gave a word to a lady who said I had got it totally wrong. I accepted that and apologised. However, the next morning she came to me and said she had not initially received what I said because she had wanted God to say something else. On taking time she could now recognise that the word was from God. Sometimes we need to give time for words to settle in our heart, but if they do not settle we can put them to one side.

4) Involving others in judging words is essential to combat our subjectivity, independence and isolation tendencies. We are a family and sharing words with close friends or those we are in a discipleship relationship with opens us up for wisdom and counsel. They can also cheer us on and keep us persevering in waiting for a fulfilment, as they remind us of things God has said when we have perhaps lost heart or grown weary. Involving others is important not only for words given to us as prophecy, but for things that God says to us personally which have elements of direction in. Factions and divisions occur when one person's revelation is not witnessed

by another, but no room is given for any other viewpoints. God values relationships over all things (John 17).

5) We are told in 1 John 4:1-3 (see also Matt 7:15-20) that we must test the spirits. There are three spirits; the Spirit of God, the spirit of man and the enemy. Prophecy is often a mix of our spirit and the Holy Spirit. God's intention is relationship and his purpose in communion with us is to make us more like him (2 Cor 3:18). The way gifts operate within us can be determined and shaped by our personality, those traits and characteristics that make us unique. We are also spiritual beings that have the nature and character of God indwelling us. As we learn to know ourselves and understand the operation of the Holy Spirit within us we can become clearer voices for God, in all that we say, do and are (not forgetting that Father does not only speak in words).

Testing the spirit means discerning who is behind a word, anything that feels manipulating or trying to control is not from God, as where the Spirit of God is there is liberty (2 Cor 3:17). When we are new believers or new to the gift it is probable that the spirit behind our prophetic words is mixed between our own thoughts and ideas and the Spirit of God. That is why a feedback loop is helpful so we can see what comes from us and what comes from God. This is also the case when we know the people well who we are praying and prophesying over, as it is easy for us to mix some of that knowledge with what God is saying. Therefore, it is often better to keep things short and simple, however we are not going to damage anyone from giving them encouraging words and that is why the boundaries of edification, exhortation and comfort are so important.

There are individuals that have the gift of discernment of spirits (1 Cor 12:10) and this gift is specifically useful if a (public) word is given that does not sit comfortably with a number of people. Accurate revelation does not equal Godly character as can be seen in the examples of Balaam (Numbers 22), King Saul (1 Samuel 10:9-11), and the slave girl in Acts 16:16. There are times therefore when discerning the spirit behind the word is important to protect the church.

6) We need to judge the prophecy by the outcome. This does not necessarily mean the fulfilment of the word; some words may take a long time to reach fulfilment. Abraham is a clear example of this, it took twenty five years from when God first promised him an heir (Gen 15:1), to when Isaac was born. In the intervening years God renewed his promise on several occasions. All prophecy should however produce fruit in the life of the one to whom it is given and the one giving it, through closer relationships with Christ and giving glory and honour to God.

Walking with our words

Once a word has been given the responsibility for that word now passes to the one who has received it, and we are encouraged to mix it with our faith. Then as James instructs us we need to become more than just hearers of the word (James 1:22), *"do not merely listen to the word ... we need to do what it says"*. We are going to explore what this might mean in the rest of this chapter by considering the context into which words might be spoken and how we can respond in obedience and action. I always try and remember the lesson of Naaman in 2 Kings 5 who felt the word of the prophet was not lofty enough for him and almost missed out on his healing because he did not want to do what Elisha said.

Fortunately he had faithful friends who persuaded him to listen and obey and wash himself in the river Jordan.

Words may be for the immediate present (now words), they may be for the future (destiny words), they may be confirming words (aligning with what God has already put in our spirit or already spoken to us), or sometimes there may be an element of something new. Frequently words may be a mixture of more than one of these elements. Interpreting how words fit into the wider context of our lives is important and that is why it is so useful to keep words together, physically or electronically, in a book or folder, where they can be revisited regularly. Prophecy does not speak into a vacuum and the timing of God in fulfilling the word means that we might have to make some adjustments in our minds and hearts, as often God wants to change things in us prior to fulfilment.

Understanding God's timing is critical, but also understanding how he speaks about time is helpful. There is often a gap between when the prophecy is given and its fulfilment where we need to respond to God and walk with our prophetic word, holding on in faith. Sometimes the word may come to prepare us for a future event, but God may speak in the present tense. This is so that when that event arrives, the prophecy becomes a now word we can stand on. Sometimes words may take a long time to be fulfilled so we need to hold on in faith. The example in John 11 of Lazarus helps to illustrate that we do not always know the bigger picture that God is working towards. When Jesus heard about Lazarus being sick his disciples assumed that he would go and heal him, however God's intention was to raise him from the dead and so Jesus waited. Sometimes we may be waiting for a fulfilment because God has a different agenda from the one we initially perceive. A good friend of mine heard God say to her "in a year this will feel like a dream", she subsequently contracted Covid19 and was very poorly for a long period, however because God had spoken to her ahead of time she was able to hold onto the word through the difficult period.

God's word to us may be a picture of our destination, but we still have to go on a journey with him. Sometimes when we receive a word it appears that the circumstances we are in immediately challenge it. Think of Joseph and his two dreams; before they were fulfilled he ended up in a pit, being sold as a slave and being put in prison. It was not the outworking that he would have expected, however he remained faithful and eventually his dreams were fulfilled. In these instances where circumstances seem to challenge what God has said we need to fight off unbelief and discouragement, through developing an attitude of patience and perseverance (Heb 6:12). We must not allow a circumstantial challenge to rob us of the fullness God wants us to inherit. I find it helpful in times like this to turn what God has said into a prayer; "Lord you said..." One example of this relates to a good friend; about 18 years ago she got very sick while we were on holiday as families together and we left her in hospital to drive home thinking we might not see her again in this world. However, as a church we knew that she had a prophetic word over her life that she would be a "long liver". So we all went to God with this prayer. Not only did she recover on that occasion but has subsequently come through other attacks on her health.

Sometimes the words God speaks may seem impossible to us, but we need to understand the language of heaven. When God speaks the word is supposed to create something in us that is bigger than our current vision, so it is going to feel impossible without his anointing.

> "What no eye has seen, what no ear has heard and what no human mind has conceived" the things God has prepared for those who love him—these are the things God has revealed to us by his Spirit. The Spirit searches all things, even the deep things of God. (1 Cor 2:9-10).

If we look at the figures in the Bible they were often given assignments bigger than them, because God wants to demonstrate who he is and his nature, strength and provision, not just to us but to the world around us. The language of faith is not always logical or rational because heaven sees everything as possible and the prophetic encourages us to join with heaven and think in a positive way. *"God who....calls those things which do not exist as though they did"* (Romans 4:17). Graham Cooke teaches that negativity is an earthly mindset, so if we are feeling negative we need to "have another thought" because of who God is and his heart towards us. The kindness of God means that destiny or life words are sometimes repeated and confirmed, to help keep us pressing on to fulfilment. Having a heart of thanksgiving is a powerful tool in seeing the word fulfilled, especially if we celebrate what we can see happening as the prophecy unfolds. Just as many of the prophecies in the Old Testament were layered, they had a meaning for then but also a meaning for the future, our words may contain more than we can currently see.

When God speaks the word is designed to create something in us that is bigger than our current vision.

One of the biggest obstacles we often face in seeing our prophecies fulfilled is that we do not live out of our God given identity. Think about the twelve spies who went into Israel and came back, ten reported they *seemed like grasshoppers in their own eyes"* (Numbers 13:33) and subsequently never entered the fullness of God's promises. The reality of living in the fulfilment of what God says is that sometimes we have to act as if the words are true and work at changing our view of ourselves by agreeing with what God has said. One of the ways we can do this is by making decrees and declarations.

Declarations and decrees

Paul encourages Timothy to take prophecy seriously and use it as a weapon to fight God's battles (1 Tim 1:18). Paul's exhortation to Timothy to use his prophetic words to fight with does not talk about what specific battles these are, but often the battle we have to face is for God's truth and the renewing of our mind. Jesus called the devil the father of lies (John 8:44) and prophetic words and encouragement are one of the weapons that can defeat lies that the enemy would try to upset and destroy with. The Bible tells us that the power of life and death is in the tongue (Proverbs 18:21, James 3:3-5) so what we speak can change things. We only have to look at Genesis 1 and how God spoke the world into being to get a sense of the power behind God's words. We can also look at examples like Ezekiel (37:1-14) in the valley of dry bones to see that through the Spirit our words can speak life.

Psychology also demonstrates how the power of language can impact a person's self-worth and there have been many theories on the power of labelling and self-belief. It is not difficult to find studies and ideas related to the power of words to do harm or good with a quick internet search. The brain uses repetition to learn and is always searching for patterns and consistency, so phrases spoken, heard or used over and over start to form patterns of belief. It is why we are encouraged to focus on and think about positive things (Phil 4:8). Engaging with scripture, worship and prophetic words regularly and intentionally is therefore part of how we can renew our minds (Romans 12:2). Meditation is a part of what we can do, and Mary provides a good example as she *"treasured these things and pondered them in her heart"* (Luke 2:19). Forgetting or neglecting to engage with what God says can impact the way what God has said is fulfilled, so in engaging with the words he has spoken we are co-labouring with him.

I believe when God speaks to our identity he wants us to see that word become part of us, so turning it into a declaration or decree is really powerful, particularly if we use it regularly in our devotions. A decree is *"an official order that has the force of law,"* and Ecclesiastes 8:4 says: *"where the word of the king is, there is power".* As we agree with what God's word calls us to be, and appropriate its truth, God works the transformation in us through the Holy Spirit.

Our decree is *prophetic* when it begins in God's intention that has been revealed through the Holy Spirit. We then have authority on earth to apply the Father's plans through the agreement of our own words. *"You will also decree a thing, and it will be established for you; and light will shine on your ways."* (Job 22:28, NASB). Decrees can be personal and corporate. In our church we have corporate declarations from our prophetic words on our walls which we use as part of our services and prayer. They have become a statement of the vision of the church and God's heart and purposes for our city.

Making decrees is not just about repeating words or a formula, it is about understanding who we are and where we are speaking from, 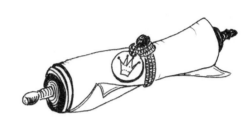 that we are seated in heavenly places (Eph 2:6) and therefore this is where the authority comes from. We do not always need to speak loudly in order for a declaration to be effective, but we should say them out loud so that we hear them as well, as faith comes by *"hearing..the word of God"* (Romans 10:17). Having them somewhere that is easily seen e.g. a notice board, by a computer, on a mirror, by our bed, allows us to regularly repeat them.

Activities to develop decrees

Using scripture

One way of starting to think about decrees is by using scripture, which we are told is a weapon (Eph 6:17) that we have been given and is one that will strengthen our faith (Romans 10:17).

Start by choosing one or two verses that

- God has spoken to you through, or

- That have a prophetic meaning for you (i.e. relates to

something God has spoken in prophetic word),or

- You would like to apply by faith to a particular situation.

The first step is to personalise it by changing it so it speaks in the first person. This might mean you also need to slightly adapt the wording. If you also change the tense to the present tense it can add more power to a personal declaration.

A simple example is Ex 14:13 and Psalm 46:10 (*Be still and know that I am God*) , this could become: (I decree) I know how to rest in God and meet with Him in that place of peace.

Another example that I use is Nehemiah 8:10 which says *"the joy of the Lord is your strength"*. Because I have a lot of words about joy over my life and have been given this scripture many times I combined it with a few other thoughts that had come through my prophetic words and made the following decree.

I decree that I am filled to overflowing with the joy of the Lord so that others are impacted with his joy for them. I am made to have fun, to play and include others in.

Here is an example of a decree where several different scriptures have been woven together;

God says he never gets tired or weary and gives me his strength moment by moment. He encourages me to wait and rest in his provision and then I will rise refreshed and renewed. His hand has been upon me from my mother's womb, and he has planned works for me to do in Christ that bring glory to his name. He has put a royal mantle on me to reflect my calling. I go out in his anointing. (Isaiah 40; Psalm 139; Eph 2:16; 1 Peter 2:9)

Making decrees from prophetic words.

It is my experience that prophetic words often speak into three areas: identity, giftings and callings. I look at my new words regularly and write down under each of these headings what God has said through the prophetic words I have been given. I can then see what has been emphasised and repeated even if the actual words used are slightly different. I can also then look at them alongside previous words (I do have about 35 years worth!) and see what has been fulfilled, and what I still need to bring to God.

To start writing decrees from prophetic words, I would start with the ones about identity, because it is critical that we know who we are. I have undertaken this activity several times and in doing this begun to build up a very clear picture of who God says I am.

Rather than writing "I decree"... you can start with the idea of "God says I am ...or God sees me as ..."

You can also do this with children in a more creative way for example where they create a silhouette or picture of themselves and write the words around or inside it. The more creative might like to develop watercolour or mixed media backgrounds on which to write these words God has said.

It is very helpful if these words are then put up somewhere where they can be seen and read regularly. This helps us to develop faith in what God says and allows the word to become part of who we are.

Using prophetic words in times of trouble and challenge.

Often God will speak to us ahead of time because we will need to use the word given to us as a rock to stand on when difficulties come.

In the passage in Mark's gospel where Jesus calms the sea, we have an example of how the word was already spoken because Jesus had said "let us go over to the other side"(4:35) indicating their destination. When the storm arose, the disciples forgot that God had already declared his purposes and panicked at what they saw. If we can develop an attitude that starts with what God has said about our lives and our destination rather than looking at the storm we may not feel overwhelmed by what comes our way. This is another reason why it is important to keep track of words spoken over our lives. Get in the habit of re-reading prophetic words when challenges come and then declaring or standing on what God has said.

Chapter 6

THE ANGELIC REALM AND THEIR INTERACTIONS ON EARTH

Once, when I was off work due to life stresses, I had been reading Psalm 91 many times as an encouragement that God was with me. As I lay on my bed I had the tangible sense of a large wing enfolding me from my head to my toes and being totally covered and I sensed an amazing calmness and security in being protected in this way. It only lasted moments but has been a source of comfort and reassurance ever since. This supernatural encounter enabled me to move on from the moment of darkness I was in. Supernatural encounters and the angelic realm are an important part of how heaven touches earth. I previously mentioned angels as messengers of God, as that is how we are most familiar with them in the Bible stories, but they also serve other functions in their interactions with humans. Benny Hinn suggests that the picture that Jacob had in Gen 28:11-13, when he saw the angels ascending and descending between heaven and earth indicates how they act between the two realms constantly. They move between both realms to accomplish the tasks God has for them.

Sometimes children will be far more open to the angelic realm than adults and they may see or sense angels, some children do this even before they are verbal. It is helpful to have a biblical understanding of the role and function of angels in our lives, in order to be able to guide and support children who have seen them, or had visions or dreams about them. We need to understand them as everyday occurrences in the spiritual realm rather than something to be worried or fearful about. Angels are mentioned at least 108 times in the Old Testament and 165 times in the New Testament so it is clear that they have a part to play in our engagement with heaven.

Much of what we think of when we think about angels has been informed by art, culture and the media and is therefore not necessarily accurate. The Bible informs us that angels are created beings as part of heaven's creation (Neh 9:6). Typically in western culture angels are often portrayed as beautiful creatures with wings, however many references in the Bible indicate that not all angels have wings and that they can appear like men (Acts 1:11, Heb 13:2), so that we may not even realise they were angels. A good friend believes she had an encounter with this type of angel when she had a puncture in her car on a road in rural South Africa which was not a very safe experience. Shortly after another car drew up and two men got out and fixed the wheel for her. They then drove on and when she started driving her car they were already out of sight, even though it was a long straight road ahead.

In many the biblical accounts angels can also appear as quite terrifying, as Matt 28:2-4 indicates;

There was a violent earthquake, for an angel of the Lord came down from heaven and, going to the tomb, rolled back the stone and sat on it. His appearance was like lightning, and his clothes were white as snow. The guards were so afraid of him that they shook and became like dead men.

Certainly the angelic encounters of Daniel, Ezekiel and the Book of Revelation illustrate the angelic as glorious and powerful beings who serve God. We should display a right kind of reverence towards them without worshipping them or praying to them (Rev 22:8-9).

There are different kinds of angels mentioned in scripture: specifically the cherubim, the seraphim, and the living creatures; some of these are only seen when individuals have visions of heaven. They are strange and wonderful beings and those perceiving them often use metaphors to try and explain what they looked like (Ezk 10:1-20). The first mention of cherubim is in the garden of Eden when God placed them to guard the entrance after Adam and Eve had been expelled (Gen 3: 24). Cherubim have a particular place in the history of the people of Israel and their worship. Two cherubim with large wings were designed out of gold and set upon the ark of the covenant (Ex 25: 20-22), they also appeared woven into the furnishings of the tabernacle (Ex 26:1). God communed with Moses from in between the cherubim on the ark (Ex 25:22). Seraphim are only mentioned by Isaiah and are described as the burning ones. Clearly these living creatures and angelic beings are for us to wonder at. We also know there are large numbers of them as Daniel in his vision of God on the throne describes, *"Thousands upon thousands attended him; ten thousand times ten thousand stood before him"* (see also Deut 33:2, Heb 12:22, Rev 5:1).

The main activity of the angels in heaven, which include the living creatures, appears to be praise and worship (Isaiah 6:1-3 and Revelation 4-5). It is not surprising therefore when we are in our corporate gatherings in praise and worship that individuals sometimes sense the presence of angels in the midst of the congregation. Some friends recount how they have heard angel voices joining in their worship. I remember one occasion when I sensed an angel had appeared and wanted to bring hope to individuals, many of those who went to where I sensed him felt touched and encouraged. Not all angels will appear in a form we can distinguish. John Paul Jackson explained from the verse in James 1:17 *"Every good and perfect gift is from above, coming down from the Father of the heavenly lights, who does not change like shifting shadows"*, that he had often, in his private devotion, seen moving bright lights when he sensed the presence of God. This occurred in a conference where he was speaking that I was in, where many of the congregation saw lights moving around at quite a speed over all of us. I think these encounters are usually a sign that heaven is coming closer. Peter explains that angels are intrigued by salvation (1 Pet. 1:9–12) and perhaps by looking at us and our worship of the saviour they are trying to understand the wonder of what we have received, because they can never experience salvation for themselves.

Angelic encounters can be a sign of heaven being released on earth.

Some angels also have a role to play in responding to the command of God in relation to engaging with people on the earth. Jesus says in Matthew 18:10 *"See that you do not despise one of these little ones. For I tell you that their angels in heaven always see the face of my Father in heaven."* This verse may promote the idea of guardian angels, something Jews of Jesus' time believed in. Not everyone thinks this means a personal angel however, but rather that there are angels in the very presence of God who may be sent to offer help and protection if they are needed. One girl started seeing angels when she was aged about 6 or 7. She describes them as in human form but a bit indistinct and they slightly glow. They often come as a comfort to her when she is distressed as they enhance the presence of God in her life. She feels closer to God when they appear and more aware of him.

The angels that appear to men and women on the earth seem to have several functions; including guidance, protection and deliverance. Hebrews 1:14 declares *"Are not all angels ministering spirits sent to serve those who will inherit salvation?"* Perhaps we are more familiar with their role as messengers from God because of the Christmas story. The Greek word 'angelos' means "messenger" or "one who brings a message" and is therefore often translated as angel, although it can also be used to refer to human messengers. The biblical authors use of 'angelos' when recounting angelic appearances can be seen to indicate that a task of these supernatural creatures is to bring a message from God. We have the angel of the Lord who visited Zechariah (Luke 1:11), Gabriel who visited Mary (Luke 1:26), the angel in Joseph's dreams (Matt 1:20; Matt 2:13) and the angelic host that visited the shepherds (Luke 2:10).

Angels also appeared to the apostles with messages as in the example in Acts 27:23-24. Here the message from the angel to Paul, was also a promise and encouragement for the rest of the people on the ship, as during the storm he told them everyone would survive the impending shipwreck. In Acts 8:26 an angel came to Philip to guide him, through a message, to go and meet the Ethiopian eunuch. In Acts 10 Cornelius a devout God fearing man was sent an angel in a vision who gave him clear directions. So we can see from these examples that angelic messengers were active in the early church giving different kinds of messages and direction. It is valuable to also consider the other activities that angels may undertake, so that we may be open to how they may minister to individuals and the body of Christ.

Provision. In three places in the Bible God uses angels to provide for physical needs; such as a well of water for Hagar when she had been cast out from the family of Abraham (Genesis 21:17-20), and food for Elijah while he was journeying to Horeb (1 Kings 19:6). There were even angels who came to Jesus after his temptation who strengthened and encouraged him (Matthew 4:11).

Protection. There are some well known Bible passages where we see God sending his angels to protect and keep people out of physical danger. Two of these occur in the book of Daniel. In Daniel 3, Shadrach, Meshach and Abednego were tossed into a fiery furnace for failing to bow down and worship a statue of the king. The Bible describes the event and portrays a fourth man walking with them who protects them from damage. Then in Daniel 6, Daniel is thrown into the pit of lions and we are told that God sent an angel and shut the mouths of the lions.

There are also many psalms that promote the idea of God's angels as beings who protect and rescue. Psalm 34:7 talks about "*The angel of the Lord encamps around those who fear him and rescues them*". Psalm 91:11-13 also offers us a picture of God's protection through angels,

For he will command his angels concerning you
to guard you in all your ways;
they will lift you up in their hands,
so that you will not strike your foot against a stone.

While we may not always see the angels with us, we can be confident that God sends them when necessary as illustrated by the story of Elisha and his servant (2 Kings 6:7) when they were surrounded by an enemy army that had come to capture them. Elisha prays for the servant's eyes to be opened to see into the heavenly realm and he "*saw the hills full of horses and chariots of fire all around Elisha.*" They were already there but the servant had not been given the eyes to see them until Elisha prayed.

One of the children at church (8) recounts how God has shown her that there are angels in her room to protect her, in her own words: "*God showed me that I have 11 angels in my room, one is called Grace. A few years ago C painted a picture of an angel holding a pearl - it was a picture God had put in my head and she painted it for me and God said that's Grace... Before I got scared and thought robbers or BFG would come into my room and snatch me, but now I'm really encouraged that angels are there to protect me."* Obviously this is an encouraging account from a child of how God sought to help her through a vision of angels, it helps to illustrate how the Holy Spirit might reveal truths in a way children can understand.

Deliverance. We also have accounts in the Bible of angels rescuing God's people from trouble. In Acts 5:19 the angels released the apostles from prison and then repeated this for Peter in Acts 12. It is worth noting that this account of Peter's release from prison suggests that even though they had experienced something similar before (Acts 5) there was not an assumption that the same thing would happen again. It is also very clear in the Acts 12 account that although the church was praying for Peter they were quite surprised when he turned up at the house where they were praying. From these accounts I think it is reasonable that we should not assume, just because we pray, that God will send angels to accomplish the same task in exactly the same way. We must also remember that most of the apostles were imprisoned at some time, often before they were martyred, but God did not always send angelic helpers. However, there are occasions when our prayers may release the angelic to act on our or others behalf.

One example of this is in Daniel 9:23, Daniel was in the habit of praying three times a day in his room, and during one of these times Gabriel turned up *"As soon as you began to pray, Gabriel told him, an answer was given, which I have come to tell you"*. Then in Daniel 10:12-14 we have the account of the angel who had got delayed on his way to answer Daniel's prayer. There is not scope in this book to explore all the aspects of this event and the role of the archangel Michael in battling for the message to get through, suffice to say this is an example to help us remember Eph 6 :12 *"For our struggle is not against flesh and blood, but against the rulers, against the authorities, against the powers of this dark world and against the spiritual forces of evil in the heavenly realms"*. When considering the angelic realm it is important that what we experience and understand is rooted in biblical truth and the gift of discernment is helpful at times as we need to be aware that Satan is described in the Bible as masquerading as an angel of light (2 Cor 11:14). However, we do not need to get worried and should treat children's accounts of the angelic in a matter of fact way.

Healing. There is only one story in the Bible where an angel is specifically mentioned as being involved in healing, it is related to an angel stirring the waters at the pool of Bethseda (John 5). However, in the book of Revelation angels do many actions on God's command that involve bringing God's power in the form of fire, thunder, lightning, glory and much more. Whether angels join our meetings bringing healing is a contested area of angelic engagement in some parts of the church. However, I believe if we take Hebs 1:14 that they are ministering spirits (where the word minister means to meet the need of another), it is reasonable at times that they may be sent from God to bring healing gifts alongside the ministry of the church under the power of the Holy Spirit. Kris Vallotton teaches that it is perhaps an angel that has been released to fulfil God's word in the passage in Matt 8:5-13 because he has an understanding of the authority that exists in heaven and as we can also see in Psalm 103:20 angels are released to do God's bidding.

As these examples illustrate there is so much in heavenly realms that we know so little about, but God does send angels to earth to accomplish his purposes. We may sense they are with us (as in a vision), we may have dreams about them, or we may have met them looking like humans and not realised they were angels until later. If children are having encounters with angels we should take them seriously whether or not we have had similar experiences ourselves. Seeing an angel does not make a particular child any more special than any other and we must not over inflate certain experiences or value them more highly but give glory to God for his encountering us in different ways.

Activity: Hosting angels

It is not really possible to practice seeing angels but perhaps we can prepare our hearts and minds for them by acting in response to the verse in Hebrews 13:2 which encourages us to *"not forget to show hospitality to strangers, for by so doing some people have shown hospitality to angels without knowing it."*

How about if as a family you regularly looked round at church for visitors and agreed to invite them back to your house for a coffee or lunch after the service or meeting, perhaps once a month. It is quite possible that by responding to Paul's encouragement to look after visitors that on one occasion you might find you have hosted angels.

.

Chapter 7

LET YOUR KINGDOM COME: HEALING, SIGNS AND WONDERS

We are taught to pray let your kingdom come and sometimes we see this happen as we encounter God in the day to day. My husband had hurt his ankle while working and was having trouble walking on it. He went to lay on the sofa to rest it while I went out. While resting he listened to a podcast and as he did so the Holy Spirit met him in a very special way and revealed a deep truth to his heart. He then stood up and found that his ankle had also been healed. God meets us and the Holy Spirit works in us to bring us to wholeness in our hearts, minds and bodies. Sometimes we pray and sometimes as in the event just described God just does things when we meet with him.

Two gifts of the Spirit we have not so far talked about in the list in Corinthians are those of healing (1 Cor 12:9) and miracles (1Cor 12:10). While we might be familiar with the idea of healing, having experienced a healing encounter ourselves and heard testimonies of those who are healed, we have probably experienced far fewer examples of miracles taking place. I have been part of teams who have prayed for the multiplication of food and many more have been fed than there was food for and I have heard testimony of creative healing miracles, such as the deaf hearing from people I know who saw it happen. I know all things are possible and God is continually challenging me to align my faith with what the Bible says rather than my limited personal experience. However, I am writing in the hope and expectation that as the church we will see more people begin to move in these gifts and that we will support and encourage our children to live in the impossible as their inheritance *"Very truly I tell you, whoever believes in me will do the works I have been doing, and they will do even greater things than these, because I am going to the Father "* (John 14:12-14).

Healing

I believe it is important that we teach biblical principles about what we can expect God to do, rather than letting our possibly slight current experience be the measure of our faith. We need to keep praying and declaring and speaking the truth, as everyone I know who has a healing gift talks about how many hundreds of people they had to pray for before they saw a breakthrough. So just like the other gifts we need to keep practicing. Some individuals will have a greater anointing than others in the area of healing, but we should all be ready to see God move through us. Through the gospels we see that Jesus gave authority to his disciples to do everything that he did (Matt 10:1, 8; Luke 9:1; Mark 6:13) and this continued in the early church (Acts 3:1-10; Acts 14:8-10; Acts 28:8-9). The apostles also urged the early church to continue in this ministry (James 5:15-16; 1 Cor 14).

I think one important element here is about making it a natural everyday event to pray if someone is sick or in pain. One healing I experienced was while I was waiting with a friend in a shop. I mentioned I had a thumb I could not bend and the doctor had suggested it was the beginning of arthritis, my friend just took hold of my hand and prayed a simple prayer and immediately I could move my thumb and have not had any trouble with it since. Another testimony about prayer in the everyday comes from a child's carer who explained how she picked the child up from school. In her words *"I was coughing like in a coughing fit. I told the child I wasn't feeling great and she asked if she could pray for me. She prayed for me and after a while travelling I realised my cough had completely gone. We were both really happy about how God had answered prayer".*

When asked about praying for healing Heidi Baker responded that God has told her many times "my job is to love, his job is to heal" so even if we have not seen the healing breakthrough yet we can still stand with people who are sick in heart, soul and body and love them and continue to pray. One of the leaders in our church also remarked that God had shown him a similar idea when he confessed that he did not think he had enough faith to pray for a lame beggar in India, God told him it was not more faith he needed but more compassion. This has such resonance for me when I look at the life of Jesus. There are so many scriptures where it talks about Jesus being moved with compassion before he healed those in front of him (e.g. Matt 14:14, Matt 20:34). Given this it is clear we need not just the gifts of the Spirit but the fruit of the Spirit to move in this anointing.

We may not need more faith but more compassion.

While it is evident that Jesus followed no set formula when praying for the sick, there are various models that are regularly used in training people in how to pray, which can be a great help if you are starting on this journey. We have used the Vineyard 5 step model in our church, this model was formulated by John Wimber and is utilised by Randy Clark whose ministry Global Awakening sees many healings. Creating opportunities for children to pray

alongside others helps develop their confidence. In our church we simplified the model to help encourage children to pray by first asking the person they are praying for what is wrong, then simply getting them to pray "sickness go" and "healing come" in Jesus name. Just recently we have had two children testify to how they used this model to pray for someone. The first was when a child was praying for her mum at bedtime, who had a bad neck/shoulder and could not move it. Next day her mum got up with no stiffness or pain. Then the following week another girl told about how her cousin had been climbing a tree when the branch broke and he fell about 3 metres to the ground and hurt his back. She said she prayed, "pain go, healing come", his dad carried him back to the car and when he got there he was okay and ate cake.

After praying for somebody it is good practice to ask them if anything has happened, as they may feel a sensation such as heat on the part of the body being prayed for. If it is possible it helps to get the person being prayed for to see if God has done anything, e.g. if they had limited range of movement can they move it more now? Has the pain they were feeling decreased? They may receive some movement back immediately or they may have total healing, they may feel the pain decrease by 20% or 80%. Depending on the situation it is always good to thank God for what he has started to do and then pray again. At a recent Sunday meeting two different people gave words of knowledge (via zoom chat) about a heavy heart and a sore throat and this was the testimony received after *"I had a very heavy heart about work yesterday and a sore throat for two and a half months. I felt loved and cared for ...I didn't feel the heaviness...my throat was a bit better ...I want to praise God for healing me yesterday."* Then a few weeks later there was another word of knowledge about a bad knee, two people responded and one got healed instantly.

Giving thanks and sharing the testimonies is really important, as I previously discussed the Hebrew word testimony means 'do it again', and we are making an opportunity for God to move when we share a testimony. Obviously when we are pressing into God for healing and the miraculous we are aware that currently not every prayer is answered as we would like, or as immediately as we would want to see and we have to be ready to support children on their own journeys to avoid disappointment becoming a barrier to faith and pressing in to the promises. There are many helpful sources for thinking through some of these issues, I can recommend *God on Mute* by Pete Greig to explore the goodness of God in the midst of the battle and also Paul Mainwaring's book *Kisses from a Good God* which explores the role of medicine in the healing testimony.

Signs and wonders (miracles)

Miracles can also be thought of as signs and wonders, as one definition of a wonder *'is an event inexplicable by the laws of nature, a miracle'*. Signs and wonders are designed to point to Jesus and make us stop and respond in awe to who God is and what he is able to do. I think we often have signs that appear as small events in our lives but that can help us wonder and express gratefulness to the God who we serve and worship. An example of this that I experienced recently was where I was praying with a friend for a group who were about to go out for a session of healing on the streets. The forecast for the morning was very poor, so we asked God to hold the rain off when we worshipped, which he did and as we came to the end of the worship it started to rain. The specific timing for this answer to prayer encouraged those who had prayed as a sign that God was with them. On another occasion a friend of mine saw God turn back storm clouds after prayer, these clouds had been heading straight for where they were set up to do ministry outdoors.

Sometimes these signs are just a demonstration of God's love and kindness as happened for one boy who was looking for a new bike during lockdown. He asked his parents if he could have an orange one as it was his favourite colour. They were aware of how challenging it was to find the right kind of second hand bike without being specific as to colour, however, the only bike that was suitable and available for him was an orange one. He was obviously very blessed and testified during our meeting of God's provision. Another lady confessed that she had been anxious about finance, but then she kept finding small coins turned up on the floor and around her car. These small signs encourage our hearts and expectations for God to move in bigger ways.

> ## Recognising the small signs, encourages our hearts and expectations for God to move in bigger ways.

Even the ordinary everyday can point us to God if our hearts and spirits are open, because there is nothing God has made that cannot speak to us of who he is, and lead us to him. Perhaps the most ordinary sign is the beauty of the natural world and many of us can testify to having found God amidst his creation and in the peace of the natural world. The Bible talks about some signs as everyday occurrences for example in Genesis 1:14 *"God said let there be lights in the expanse of the sky to separate the day from the night, and let them serve as signs to mark seasons and days and years"* and in Genesis 9:12 where the rainbow is the sign of the covenant God made with every living creature on the earth. Later in Exodus the actions of God in sending the plagues and bringing his people out of Egypt are also described as signs (Ex 10:2). All signs have one thing in common: they point to God and only those that do are to be trusted (Deut 13:1-3).

John explains in his gospel how the signs that Jesus did were there so that people would believe in him, *"This is the beginning of signs Jesus did in Cana of Galilee and manifested his glory and his disciples believed in him"*. And John 20:30 *"Jesus did many other signs in the presence of his disciples...these are written that you might believe*" (John 2:11). So signs that we see and experience should help us grow in our own faith.

During the season of the outpouring of the Spirit known as the Toronto Blessing, there were regular signs of God's presence in the midst of his people, with unusual events such as people being given gold teeth. There was also the experience of some finding gemstones or gold dust appearing on hands and faces. Signs and wonders such as these may puzzle, confuse and challenge us, but Jesus also provoked this response when he walked the earth. Sometimes we may be able to understand the purpose of a sign or interpret its meaning but at other times it will remain hidden. In our church there was a season when people would often find feathers in unusual places and these were interpreted as a sign of God's presence from scriptures such as Dt 32:11 and Psalm 91, and a prophetic word that had been given to a leader which encouraged us to look out for 'feathers of faith'. They were signs for us to keep persevering in our pursuit of the things God wanted to release and to believe what he was doing.

Part of the challenge of walking in this supernatural mindset for those in the western world is that it is uncomfortable to our normal way of thinking, where we often privilege intellectual skills. We use our knowledge and understanding to inform how we perceive the world and our spiritual being is often submitted to the mind. I believe God wants to readjust us, so that our mind is submitted to the Spirit and we live from the Spirit (Gal 5:16). Signs are sometimes one way he will change our perceptions and understandings. The challenge therefore for many of us in expecting to see the impossible starts in our belief system, which is often shaped by the culture around us. In the western world we are influenced by the Plato worldview that separated out the sacred and secular elements of life and part of the work the church is called to is to cross this divide and bring heaven to earth. God wants to reveal his glory in us and through us (John 17:20-23).

God wants to reveal his glory in us and through us.

Signs can also be confirmation to us of something God has said or his promises in scripture. Many can testify of God meeting their needs by receiving the exact amount of money they needed to pay a bill for example. A good friend of ours used to travel extensively following the prompting of the Holy Spirit and God always provided the means for her air fare even though she usually did not have it when she was prompted to book the tickets. These signs enable faith to grow because they show God at work in our lives.

One of the well known stories in the Old Testament of Gideon and the fleece shows that Gideon was not reprimanded by God for asking for a sign to confirm the word he had been given.

Judges 6 : 36 -40 Gideon said to God, "If you will save Israel by my hand as you have promised— look, I will place a wool fleece on the threshing floor. If there is dew only on the fleece and all the ground is dry, then I will know that you will save Israel by my hand, as you said." And that is what happened. Gideon rose early the next day; he squeezed the fleece and wrung out the dew—a bowlful of water. Then Gideon said to God, "Do not be angry with me. Let me make just one more request. Allow me one more test with the fleece, but this time make the fleece dry and let the ground be covered with dew." That night God did so. Only the fleece was dry; all the ground was covered with dew.

I do not think this example should be used to suggest we should be asking God for signs to confirm every word he gives us, as Gideon had after all been asked to go and save Israel which was a fairly big request! But I think we can have confidence that God will confirm things for us and may use a variety of ways to do it, we just need to be open.

Another definition of sign is an act or gesture used to convey an idea. Scripture is full of examples of prophets who also acted as signs as well as speaking out God's word by carrying out God ordained actions e.g. Jeremiah buys a field (Jer 32:6); Hosea marries a prostitute (Hosea 1:2), Ezekiel lies on his side (Ez 4) and Agabus ties up Paul (Acts 21:11). So we can see signs in things people do in response to God's words and I have been part of intercession and prophetic teams where we have also been led by the Holy Spirit to carry our prophetic actions such as pouring out oil, water and wine on the land. Sometimes corporately we will be led to respond to God's word as a prophetic sign or action. I remember one meeting where everyone made giant paper chains and then we broke them off people as a prophetic action of God breaking people free.

So signs can be encountered in our lives as answers to prayer, as the generous outworking of God's presence to confirm his words to us, as a response to things he has said and as things that make us wonder in awe at the bounty and majesty of the God we serve. We obviously do not seek signs for the signs sake, as we are told to seek God and his kingdom and preach the gospel but that when we do this we are promised we shall see signs following (Mark 16:17).

CONCLUSION

My hope when I started this book was that it would serve as a helpful guide for those seeking to support children in developing their relationships with God, specifically through learning how to hear God. I have always taken seriously the responsibility I have as a member of the body of Christ to use the talents God has given me in all the ways I can. Having found that in recent years my work has been with children and those caring for and teaching them, it was a logical step to consider how I could communicate some of the truths I have gained about moving in spiritual gifts, so others outside of my local church body could access them.

As I said at the beginning I am not promoting these ideas as my own, they have been utilised by many over the years in different ways and some I practiced when I was developing the gift myself. I am grateful to God that I had this opportunity to be taught and mentored, especially in the gift of prophecy, and to work with others across different churches and streams in exploring how creativity and the prophetic can work together. I was fortunate to have the opportunity to 'play' and create with the Holy Spirit as I grew in the gift and I hope you have been encouraged to consider your own growth in these gifts as well as helping to support the children you parent, care for or teach.

We should not expect children to do things exactly as we as adults do, but by providing places and spaces for them to practice and develop their gifts as part of the body my hope is that we will soon be learning from them as they become older teens and young adults who move into new revelation and understanding beyond where we have gone. Setting simple scriptural boundaries such as all prophetic words need to 'stir up, build up or cheer up', and practical values that we appreciate everyone's contribution and learn together through mistakes rather than waiting to be perfect, provides the healthy environment that makes growth possible.

I believe passionately that children are not just in training for growing up, but they can already be contributing members of our communities, learning as they go. So many of the testimonies you have read have come straight from the voices of children engaging in exploring the spiritual gifts they have. To get to this point required hard work and a collaborative adventure from parents, carers and the extended family of the church. It has been a learning journey for us all, that highlighted not just the enthusiasm with which children take to the notion of hearing God and responding to what he says, but that we needed to challenge the view that spiritual gifts are just for the few who are seen as 'being prophetic' or having a 'healing gift'. Many parents have expressed their delight to me that I was not only helping their children but that they have gone on this journey alongside them, learning more themselves about the spiritual gifts they can access.

I believe God loves an intergenerational church, and certainly the ideas about family that Jesus demonstrated are different from our own broken and divided society. The church has the opportunity to develop something that counters many of the experiences of family found in culture and that invites and draws all into a welcoming, accepting and loving experience of God's great family. I pray that as you grow in exploring God's gift that you will find for yourself that "everybody can play".

I would love to hear your experiences of using the activities in this book and any ways that you have worked with children to help them encounter God.

Please contact me at prophetic@citylife.org.uk the home of our prophetic community.

Printed in Great Britain
by Amazon